PIECED *Kaleidoscope* Quilt Blocks

Stunning Designs and Endless Inspiration for Fussy Cut EPP Patchwork

Lydia Cheney

Landauer Publishing

Pieced Kaleidoscope Quilt Blocks

Landauer Publishing, www.landauerpub.com, is an imprint of Fox Chapel Publishing Company, Inc.

Project Team
Acquisitions Editor: Amelia Johanson
Editor: Christa Oestreich
Designer: Wendy Reynolds
Studio Photographer: Mike Mihalo (2–3, 4–5, 7 top, 33, 47, 51, 55, 60 bottom, back cover bottom)
Proofreader & Indexer: Jean Bissell

Shutterstock used: Tomasash (6 main), Africa Studio (35 background, 41 background), Madredus (46 background, 55 background)

ISBN 978-1-63981-124-3

Library of Congress Control Number: 2025942582

Or write to:
Fox Chapel Publishing
903 Square Street
Mount Joy, PA 17552

Printed in China
First printing

FSC www.fsc.org MIX Paper | Supporting responsible forestry FSC® C016973

Contents

Introduction

About six years ago, I was inspired by a Lucy Boston English Paper Piecing (EPP) pattern I saw on Instagram. While this technique was new to me, EPP has been around for centuries. I was intrigued how, just by turning the individual fabric-covered paper pieces around, they would present a whole different look—like magic. Thanks to a love of puzzles, I began hand stitching quilt pieces together in a very complex, detailed, repetitive order, which led me to create beautiful EPP kaleidoscopes.

Kaleidoscope quilts feature repeating fabric prints that exactly mirror each other, transforming the pattern into new, stunning geometric forms. This book provides some basic formations that you can endlessly iterate on. Follow me as I break it down so you too can create beautiful, handcrafted items and fall in love with the art of EPP. I've even included a set of EPP templates at the back of the book that you can copy and use again and again, so your paper pieces can be made accurately.

After immigrating from Austria at a very young age, I've been influenced by my Austrian mother and Ukrainian father. Their heritage instilled in me the appreciation for the traditional, handcrafted clothing and surroundings of those cultures. My journey into needlework started at age 11 when my sister taught me to knit, which led to a lifelong exploration into handicrafts. With home economics in junior high school, I was learning the basics of sewing and various needlework.

As an adult, I learned that I had dyslexia. I realized how much I struggled with constant mistakes in reading instructions and measuring with traditional patchwork. I also discovered that I had to teach myself the many crafts I endeavored to accomplish through trial and error. Because of this, I was using different approaches to figure things out. Even with my struggles with dyslexia, I relied on my intuitive nature and took advantage of being very visual, finding I had the ability to create original designs. As my repertoire of handicrafts evolved over the years, about 20 years ago, I became fascinated and passionate about quilting. That love and obsession has recently been focused on modern EPP.

Working with our hands is very meditative. We can forget about the world outside and focus on what is in front of us instead of the intrusive thoughts running around in our heads. Quilting is a form of therapy for many of us along with a creative outlet. Today we have online networks to bring likeminded people together from around the world where we can make friendships, encourage one another, and enjoy the masterpieces from other creatives. But information on these sites can also be fleeting; here one minute and then replaced with something else in a blink. The opportunity to share my kaleidoscope EPP processes with you in this book gives me the joy of presenting a physical product that creatives can consult and use again and again to bring these magical blocks into their quilting repertoire.

What is Kaleidoscope Quilting?

Makers have pieced fabric together for a very, very long time, and so there is little that is actually new; and by new, I mean a technique that has been coined in this century. "Kaleidoscope" very well may fall into this category.

English paper piecing (EPP) began back in the 1700s in, of course, England. Since then, EPP has evolved throughout the years with a new resurgence a mere 20 years ago due to the Dutch quilt designer Willyne Hammerstein, who introduced this style of patchwork to the mainstream quilting audience in her debut book *Millefiori Quilts*, released in 2011. (Millefiori is an Italian glassmaking technique. Think of those spherical paperweights that were popular in the 1950s with glass rods arranged symmetrically inside.) To create her quilts, which are true works of art, she perfectly fussy cuts and hand pieces units together into individual blocks—perhaps "rosettes" is a better term—using diamonds, triangles, pentagons, hexagons, and other repeating geometrical shapes. The effect is breathtaking.

As more quilters dabbled in this stunning EPP effect using heavily detailed and colorful fabrics along with precision fussy cutting, the term "kaleidoscope EPP" developed. It's easy to see why. If you ever looked through a child's kaleidoscope (a heavy cardboard tube that rotates on the end to create colorful symmetrical patterns), you understand the connection.

The view through a kaleidoscope (above) shows a repeating geometric pattern. Using EPP and bold prints (left), this same effect can be achieved for a quilt.

Each of these kaleidoscope blocks are a masterpiece on their own; when brought together, it's hard to look away from all the tiny details!

A hinged mirror is a handy shortcut to picturing a kaleidoscope block before you cut.

Kaleidoscope goes hand in hand with fussy cutting. The key is to select motifs and designs that repeat/mirror as you build the design essentially in the round. Just like mirrors are used with colorful beads inside the tube to create the kaleidoscope effect, quilters use a hinged mirror standing perpendicular to the fabric to determine how to fussy cut the various units they will prepare and join using traditional EPP techniques. Depending on the complexity and layout of the pattern, the fabric designs transform into a whole new design. Just turning a few pieces around in another direction will give it a whole different look. It's magical!

Prints are also another major factor in achieving a kaleidoscope effect. The repetition looks most impressive with a recognizable pattern, and the busyness adds to the effect of a complex design—with simple techniques on your end! The use of prints is discussed more on page 17.

Once you master the technique, you'll be able to make endless combinations of kaleidoscope blocks. These can then be turned into larger projects, like a quilt, where the effect of so many blocks together creates something truly captivating!

Tools for English Paper Piecing

After working with EPP for several years and stitching thousands of pieces together to make quilts, I have found these tools to be useful. Some tools are my favorites that I can't do without. I encourage you the try these to see what works best for you.

NEEDLES

EPP requires a long, skinny needle with a sharp point. Since you are taking many tiny bites of the folded fabric edge, typically 15 stitches per 1" (2.5cm), you want a needle that pierces the fabric and slides through with little resistance. What I recommend are appliqué or milliner's needles in sizes 8–10. This will be your main tool to work with, so try different ones to see what size is comfortable in your hand. I personally like Tulip, John James, and Clover brands. There are others, so try them and find what works for you.

THIMBLE

I have to confess, I am not a thimble user; however, many EPP enthusiasts do find them helpful to reduce finger stress. There are many different types, from ergonomic rubber models to classic dimpled metals, so I recommend testing a variety and landing on what is most comfortable to you.

Although I don't use a thimble when working EPP, if I do pierce my finger with a needle, I will use a plastic dot or disk and cover it with a finger cot or blister bandage. This way, I can continue to stitch while allowing my fingertip to heal.

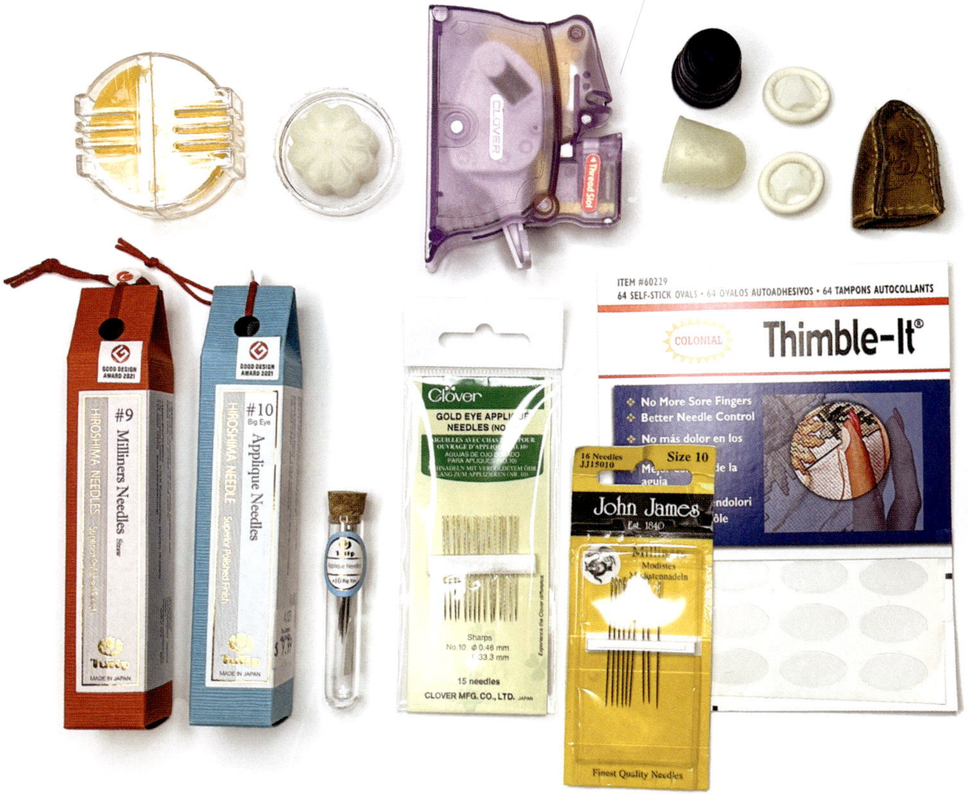

Top row: Beeswax for thread and thimble options. Bottom row: A variety of needles and another thimble option.

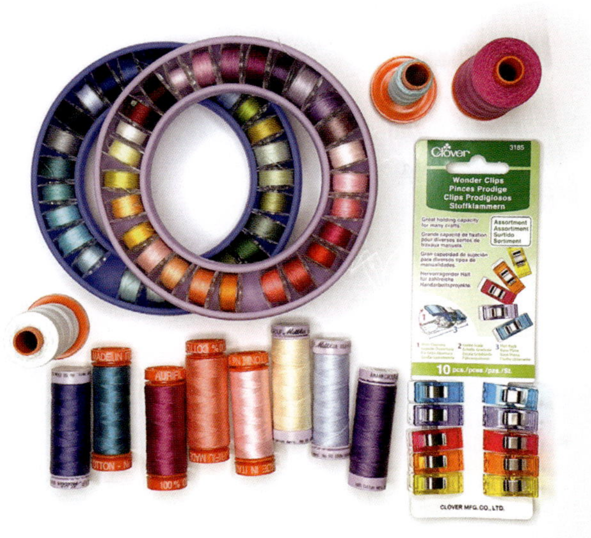

Use cotton thread when stitching on cotton fabric and polyester thread for polyester fabric. Sewing clips are best for temporarily holding EPP pieces together.

Quality scissors come in all shapes and sizes. Rotary cutters also come in different sizes.

THREAD

I have found that thread has become a controversial issue and a personal choice—cotton verses polyester versus a blend. I was shadowing a quilt appraiser for a time to gain some insight on fibers and dyes in quilt making. One thing I learned is to use cotton thread when stitching on cotton fabric, to use polyester thread for polyester fabric, and so on. Threads have different strengths and wear at different paces. Polyester thread is stronger than cotton and will eventually rub and eat away at the cotton fibers over time.

For EPP, I use a fine-quality cotton thread with cotton fabric, as they wear at the same pace. I'm spending a considerable amount of time and effort to stitch a quilt by hand, so I want it to last a long time without falling into shreds before my grandchildren get to enjoy it.

My preference is Aurifil or Mettler thread in 50wt, as I also use this weight when machine piecing. Some people use a finer thread (80wt), which is wonderful, and the stitches do tend to disappear with this option. (As you may have determined, the higher the number, the finer the weight.) However, I have a difficult time with 80wt, as it tends to break more easily and sometimes shreds. Please choose what works for you and gives you the outcome that you desire.

I also coordinate the thread color with my fabric. The thread appears to melt into the fabric and becomes close to invisible. I like matchy-matchy. I've found that quilt judges also like that for quilts that are made for show competitions.

Along with the cotton thread, I like to use a thread conditioner, usually 100% beeswax. It keeps the thread from tangling or knotting up too much. Keep your thread length to about 16"–18" (40.6–45.7cm); otherwise, it will weaken and break easily due to making too many stitches with the same fiber.

SCISSORS AND ROTARY CUTTERS

I use quality scissors in a few different sizes, and I make sure to mark them "fabrics" or "paper." I also use two rotary cutters, one for fabric and one for paper, appropriately marked. Always stick to using the correct tool on the labeled material. Paper dulls a blade more than fabric, so using the wrong blade could result in a messy cut.

When it's time to replace the blade in the fabric rotary cutter, I will put the used blade into the paper rotary cutter. I keep rotating blades to prolong their use.

GLUE

There are two ways to baste in EPP, glueing or stitching (see page 22). For glue basting, I only use slim glue pens with refills (there are lots of quilt- or sew-specific brands), which give me greater control over where I apply glue. A glue pen is low-tack and water-soluble, so it does not ruin the fabrics.

Because of the low cost, I have also tried school glue sticks that some quilters suggest. They are less expensive and designed to be used in grade school for children's projects. Personally, I have found them to be a horrible mess for EPP. I end up applying too much glue and have a terrible time removing the papers afterward. Regrettably, many people are turned off from EPP for this reason. If you're a fan of traditional glue sticks, which can be challenging due to the circumference of the glue, you might want to purchase special tips that fit directly on the end of standard glue sticks to narrow the glue line.

Once you master the control of thinner glue sticks and the amount of glue to use, then by all means, use whichever method gives you the best results.

There is a difference between glue sticks, which are a paste, and a liquid glue. Glue sticks are used to adhere EPP papers to fabric, whereas liquid glue like Elmer's glue or Roxanne Glue-Baste-It is used to adhere or baste fabric to fabric (see the Sarafina Quilt on page 54). Liquid glue basting eliminates the need to use pins.

OTHER NOTIONS

Sewing Clips—I'm always using sewing clips to hold the paper pieces together when I'm stitching them. I find Clover Wonder Clips useful because they come in different sizes.

Sewing Pins—Select pins that are easy to pick up, have nice sharp points, and in a length that is adequate for quilting. It's important in quilting for pins to be heat resistant so they won't fuse onto your ironing surface or fabric when touched by an iron.

Fabric Marking Tool—There are several kinds of markers that are designed for fabric and make temporary marks. Chalk markers will leave lines that remove over time and from touch, so be careful touching your pieces. Fabric markers, pens, and pencils can stay on fabric until the point you determine: marks from water-soluble options can be washed away and heat-erasable marks just need the hot air from a hair dryer. However, you should test markers ahead of time to make sure you can remove the markings from fabrics. Use caution when using Pilot FriXion pens because the ink does not always wash out of fabric.

Permanent Marker—Use a Sharpie or similar marker to make guidelines on acrylic templates for fussy cutting. These marks can come off easily with a cotton pad and rubbing alcohol.

Hera Marker—These tools are great for removing the papers from the fabric. I prefer the one from Clover. A big cuticle stick works well also. Just make sure whatever you use does not poke holes in your fabric as you remove the papers.

Hinged Mirror—This is a must for me. It's basically two mirrors taped together along one edge. When I hold the mirror on the fabric along with a template, it shows me a secondary pattern that I could use to fussy cut. I'm essentially giving myself a preview before I cut into the fabric.

Quilt Ruler—A clear, straight 18" (45.7cm) ruler is simply a must for every quilting room. It provides an edge for guiding your rotary cutter.

Self-Healing Rotary Cutting Mat—A self-healing cutting mat is essential for all quilting types to serve as your cutting surface when using a rotary cutter.

Fabric Starch Spray—Like glue, using spray starch (or a similar product like Mary Ellen's Best Press) is a preference. I like to wash, dry, and press my fabrics so they are nice and crisp before

Another benefit to EPP is that it doesn't require a lot of large tools or materials.

I set out examining the nuances of the print. I also use it on the EPP pieces to ensure they hold their shape after I remove the papers.

Heavy-Duty Template Plastic—If you're making your own templates (see page 19), I recommend a heavy-duty plastic. In my opinion, Dritz is the best choice. However you can always buy precut acrylic templates and precut papers, if available (see page 13).

Craft Paper—This can also be used to make your own templates. Paper is measured by weight. The average copy paper is typically 20–22 lb. (9.1–10kg) and very lightweight. Cardstock is heavier at 60–65 lb. (27.2–29.5kg). I have found that anything heavier (thicker) than 60–65 lb. (27.2–29.5kg) is too cumbersome to use. I go to an office-supply store to get a ream of craft specialty paper at 40 lb. (18.1kg). It's not as light as copy paper but not as heavy as cardstock. It feeds through my copy machine easily, and I'm able to reuse the templates up to three times.

Washi Tape—This is a narrow paper tape that can be purchased at any craft store. I use washi tape on my templates to frame the template seam allowances.

Iron and Ironing Board—A good iron is an essential investment if you quilt or sew. A steam iron aids in removing wrinkles out of fabrics. I like to lightly starch and iron all my fabrics before I even decide what to cut. Ironing is using the motion of gliding the iron back and forth, which can also stretch the fabric. However, pressing is lifting the iron in an up and down motion. For EPP, I do not use steam on paper pieces. After basting the pieces, I do press each piece to give it a nice flat edge to stitch on. I like to starch and iron all my fabrics before I even decide what to cut.

Thread Conditioner—Running stitching thread lightly through beeswax or a thread conditioner smoothens the fibers (meaning less fuzz), alleviates tangling, and some even think it makes the stitches lie flatter. If you're in a pinch and don't have any handy, try an uncolored, unflavored lip balm. You'll be doing a lot of stitching in EPP, and I think you'll find there is a difference between waxed and unwaxed thread.

Stuffing and Pillow Inserts—Premade pillow forms are available in craft and sewing stores, coming in various sizes. Consider the size of your form when you design your pillow cover. You can also make your own using basic cotton fabric for the cover filled with a polyester fiber stuffing, which is a less expensive option.

Tip

English Paper Piecing is a great craft for traveling. You can prep all your paper pieces along with a few supplies in a project bag or an organizer bin for your on-the-go projects.

Choosing a Pattern

I will begin with please, please, please don't choose a complex pattern (shape), thinking you can learn EPP as you go along. As a beginner, choose something simple like hexagons. I also recommend choosing a small project to complete in a short amount of time. Learn your skills while enjoying the process. Admire your first finished project with glee! Tell yourself that you accomplished this!

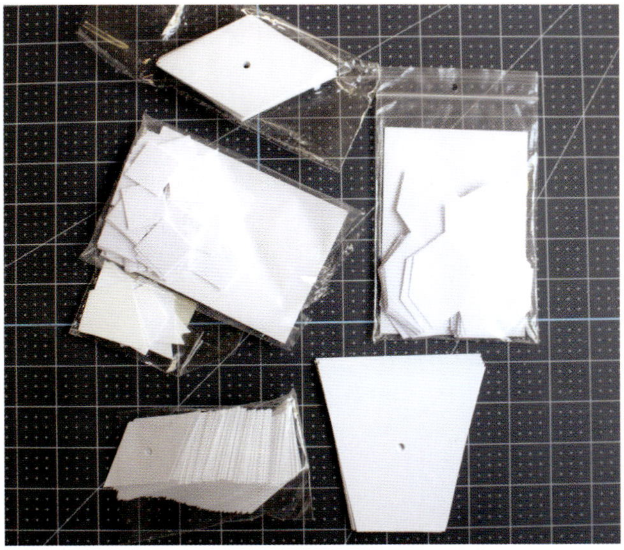

Premade paper templates can be purchased if you don't want to cut your own.

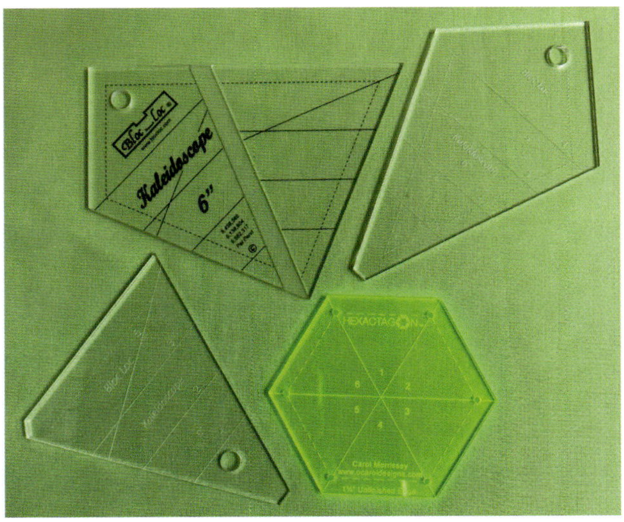

Acrylic templates come in traditional EPP shapes and sizes.

Tip

There are several places to purchase precut shapes in bulk. Always check the measurements of the EPP shapes to make sure they are correct.

How many times have you picked up a queen-sized quilt project only to throw it down, discouraged that it did not quite come together as you thought, and it ends up sitting on the shelf or left in the closet for years. No one climbs a tall mountain on their first try without training. Give yourself some grace, and be patient with yourself when learning something new. Everyone learns at their own pace and processes new information uniquely. As you learn new skills, it will become easier to complete more complex patterns or even design your own.

Select a pattern that comes with clear instructions and acrylic templates. Some patterns also come with a coloring page for you to practice the layout. Today, many EPP patterns also include reuseable, precut papers for each shape you need. You can purchase them separately for English paper piecing. This eliminates the need to trace and cut out your own, which saves time and ensures accuracy.

If making your own shapes (see page 20), you need to be very precise with your cutting skills. Accuracy is critical in EPP. The shapes are measured along the length of one side, and curved pieces are measured by height.

As you begin EPP, try a simple design like these adorable birds and add a few accompanying fabrics.

A beautiful riot of colors and designs that are exciting to fussy cut, which all come from one collection of fabrics.

Fabric Choices

If you are new to quilting, you probably need to purchase the fabrics for a project. If you've been quilting for some time, you most likely have a wonderful stash of fabrics to access. We are all drawn to fabrics that appeal to us: certain colors that we like, the allover pattern, flowers, designs, or motifs like recurring distinctive forms, shapes, or figures. Fussy cutting (see page 20) these elements can make for an even more interesting and eye-catching kaleidoscope quilt.

You may also choose solids, stripes, or dots. Let's not forget about the scale of the print, value, and contrast. As you look over your stash of fabrics, there may also be colors lacking or design elements that you have never tried. This will give you an opportunity to try something different to stretch you out of your comfort zone.

All these elements will add interest to your EPP blocks. You choose what appeals to you. All my students leave my class saying that they will never see fabrics the same way again.

I also love a scrappy quilt, which does not match specific designs like a fussy cut quilt. Making a scrappy EPP quilt is a great way to use up all your leftover scraps from previous patchwork quilt projects. I personally use up as much of the fabric as I can—no scraps left behind—or pass it on to someone else who can use it.

TO WASH OR NOT TO WASH?

This is a very subjective matter when it comes to fabric. Personally, I wash all my fabrics when they come through the door. I have ruined a quilt or two because the colors ran or bled into the other fabrics after it was complete. I have spent plenty of money and a lot of time, especially hand stitching on my quilts. Some I consider heirlooms. I don't want them to be ruined by the colors bleeding in the wash no matter the amount of color catchers, cold water, or mild soap I use. Reds, blues, and purples are the colors that run most often.

Most fabrics and batting will shrink when laundered. Someone told me once that they like that crinkle effect of the quilt when it shrinks

I use starch spray after I wash my fabric to achieve a similar crispness to unwashed fabric.

in the wash. Other people find it easier to cut unwashed fabric; they like the crispness. We all have our preferences.

After I wash my fabrics using mild soap and warm water, I will remove the fabrics after the spin cycle, trim up the ends, and fold them until I'm ready to iron them. I let them air-dry till slightly damp and iron them with some fabric starch.

It is at this point when I get a really close look at all the detail of what's printed on the fabric. I find it helpful to give each cut a good visual once-over to see the possibility and potential of what to use in my quilt.

HOW MUCH FABRIC DO I NEED?

In my class, I'm often asked, "How much fabric do I need for my project?" The amount of fabric that's needed depends on the complexity of the printed fabric and pattern you choose and thus the following:

- How many units are needed.
- How many repeats are needed in one unit.
- How far apart the repeats are on the fabric.
- How large the designs are on the fabric. (Determining how far apart the image/motif is located within a piece of fabric will give you an idea of how much fabric you need.)
- How large you want to make your project.

For Example

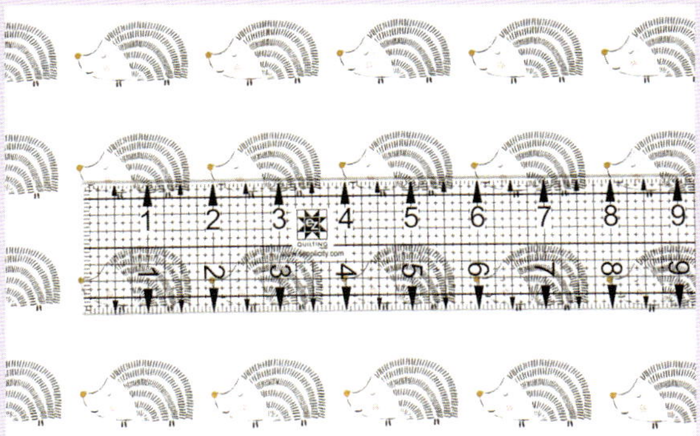

If your image/motif repeat is 2" (5.1cm) with an allover pattern, you will only need about 12" (30.5cm) of fabricto cut out six exact shapes.

If the image is 6" (15.2cm) apart, about a fat quarter of fabric should be enough to cut out six exact shapes.

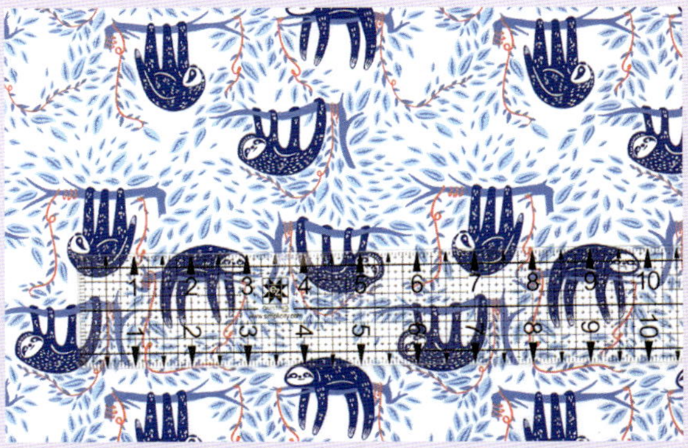

If the image/motif repeat is 7" (20.3cm) apart, you will need about a fat quarter just to be able to cut out six exact shapes.

If the image/motif repeat is 12" (30.5cm) apart, you would need up to ½ yard (45.7cm) or more of fabric to cut out six exact shapes.

Fabric collections are an easy way to find fabrics with colors and motifs that work together. Also keep an eye on the designer's other work because it is possible those may match as well.

Depending on the number of units in your pattern, how many repeats are needed in each unit equals the (estimated) amount of fabric you will need. When I am shopping for fabric, I will open the bolt up on the counter just to tally the repeats and get a good look at all the details. With time, you will develop an eye for the possibilities.

When I begin a new project, such as a bed-size quilt, I generally choose to get a ½ yard (45.7cm) bundle from a collection by one of my favorite fabric designers. I like working with a designer's collection because of their artistic style and the color palette. I also love that they have done most of the work for me in designing the beautifully artistic main fabric along with a supporting cast of fabrics that coordinate in three or more distinctive colorways. When I use a specific designer collection, I know there are as many as 12 to 30 fabrics that coordinate very well together, so I don't have to use up my time hunting for coordinates.

When fabric designers use a cohesive color palette again and again when designing their other collections, it also allows all their collections to blend well together, so I end up building a wonderful stash of fabrics I can return to again and again.

CONSIDERATIONS FOR KALEIDOSCOPE QUILTS

Fussy cutting prints is what transforms regular EPP into kaleidoscope EPP. Having a bold, recognizable motif repeating over and over again makes the design work. This helps the eye make sense of a block while also making it appear to be a more complicated design than it really is. Some of my blocks are only made of a central piece and one row around it, but that can look like an impressive geometric design thanks to the print.

When thinking about what fabric to use for a kaleidoscope block, I typically start with one that features a large print that has pieces I can single out through fussy cutting. A flower, an animal, a paisley, or another interesting shape will serve as inspiration for the surrounding pieces. These work best for larger EPP shapes but can be used anywhere. Experiment and see what you like!

Directional prints are another important source for kaleidoscope EPP. These can emphasize the geometric form, adding a flow from the center to the edges of the block or around the block. They can also work as a contrast; if you want to emphasize a certain row or shape within the block, a directional print can break up a detailed print by serving as a visual separator. This can also work in reverse.

Solids can come into play, but I rarely use them in my blocks. I use these as a background fabric, border, etc. However, I find that prints successfully carry the kaleidoscope design all the way to the edge of the piece.

Remember that the most important factor in choosing a print is that you have enough repeats of a certain motif for the EPP layout you are making. For example, projects in this book may call for six or eight of the same image; another may only need four. However, you could intentionally make some different depending on the direction (a flower facing left and right to emphasize another piece), or slight variations in the print (two different mushrooms you want to feature), or for a little visual interest. I suggest you consider these exceptions to the rule. If the differences stand out too much, your kaleidoscope loses its effect.

These two blocks show how you can use the same shapes and fabrics but get different results when focusing on other sections of fabric.

I love how the pattern of the stylized flower creates the image of fans around this block, giving it movement.

Tip

Some fabrics have such a complex print that I can find many different pieces to pull out. I might use the same fabric for all the EPP shapes in a block. This is a double benefit, because it makes the color palette easy!

A variety of blocks using the same paper shapes but different fabrics. You can get such variety depending on your fabric and what you fussy cut.

Basics of English Paper Piecing

English paper piecing (EPP) is a technique of combining small, geometric pieces of fabric together to create a larger design. It's kind of like a puzzle. Knowing the right techniques turns an intimidating project into something simple and fun.

Templates

English paper piecing requires small shapes to be made individually and then stitched together to create large, geometric designs. As you can imagine, that requires each piece to be very precise; otherwise, they won't connect properly and it throws off the shape. But another concern with kaleidoscope quilts is guaranteeing that patterns match one another. That's why templates are a mandatory part of EPP.

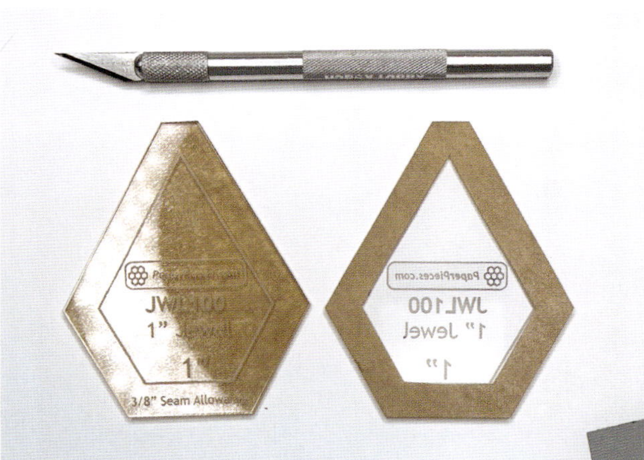

Precut acrylic templates come with a backing; I cut away only the center, leaving the seam allowance covered and using it to frame the template.

Templates that I use come in two forms:

1. Acrylic precut templates that are made to order. I get mine with a 3/8" (1cm) seam allowance. Use this to draw the outline of the shape onto the fabric that you will cut out. They are a good investment because they are easier to use and can last forever.
2. Smaller paper templates that match the finished size. Use this inside each EPP piece to hold the shape while sewing everything together. It gets removed later. Depending on the weight of the paper, you may only be able to use it once; sometimes I get multiple uses out of one.

While I recommend buying acrylic templates (see page 13), sometimes that isn't possible. For example, the Sarafina Quilt (page 54) uses a large frame piece that you could not easily find in stores or online. In this case, you must make your own template using mylar plastic. With heavy-duty mylar plastic that you can purchase in a large sheet, you can cut out any shape you want. I have provided templates at the back of this book (see page 67) for you to use, giving you a chance to try the process.

Once your acrylic and paper templates are prepared, they can be used to fussy cut with a few other tools.

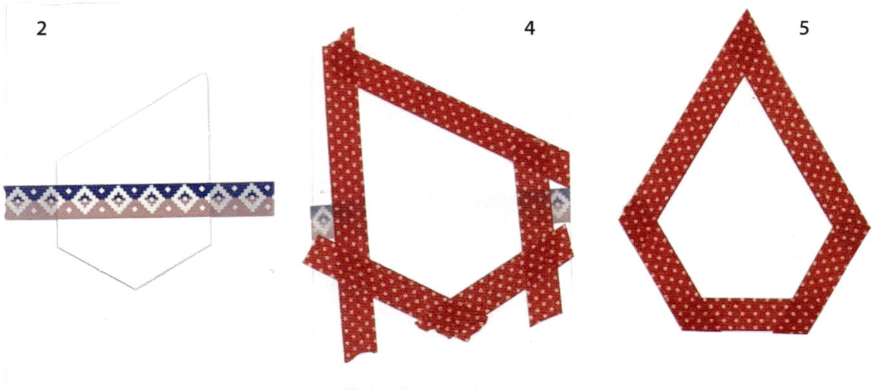

Use washi tape to frame the seam allowance on your mylar plastic template.

I made my first templates out of cardboard (yes, I was self-taught). However, when I designed my first pattern, I used heavy-duty template plastic. The example below supposes you are using plastic, but you could also use a heavier paper.

1. Trace the shape you want to use (hexie, diamond, etc.) onto paper and cut it out
2. Tape the paper shape to one side of the template plastic.
3. Turn it over. Using washi tape, lay one strip along one edge and cut the tape.
4. Move on to the next edge. Lay a strip along that edge, cut, and continue around the shape until it is encircled with the tape.
5. Remove the paper shape. Cut out the plastic shape on the outside edge of the tape. The shaded area is the seam allowance.

I use washi tape like a frame on a window. For paper pieces smaller than 1" (2.5cm), I use ¼" (6.4mm) tape; for paper pieces over 1" (2.5cm), I use ⅜" (1cm) tape. I prefer a ⅜" (1cm) seam allowance for the fudge factor when fussy cutting. It gives me that little bit of extra room if my cutting is off a bit.

Fussy Cutting

Fussy cutting is a technique where you cut out a specific pattern, motif, or design element from the fabric that you want to highlight. This can be used as a singular focal point in a quilt block or as a repeat to create a kaleidoscope effect.

I will be teaching you how to meticulously fussy cut the repeats within the fabric to use for an English paper piecing pattern to give you the kaleidoscope effect.

Heather Ross designs some fun fabrics that are great to practice fussy cutting.

FUSSY CUTTING EXERCISE

The following exercise will guide you through locating a design to fussy cut and the repeats that are needed for the kaleidoscope effect.

FOR THIS PRACTICE LESSON, I WILL BE USING:

- 1" (2.5cm) jewel-shaped paper piece with coordinating template
- Plain piece of paper
- Pencil
- Paper scissors
- Pressed fabric
- Cutting mat (optional)
- Hinged mirror
- Permanent marker
- Fabric marking tool (optional)
- Fabric scissors

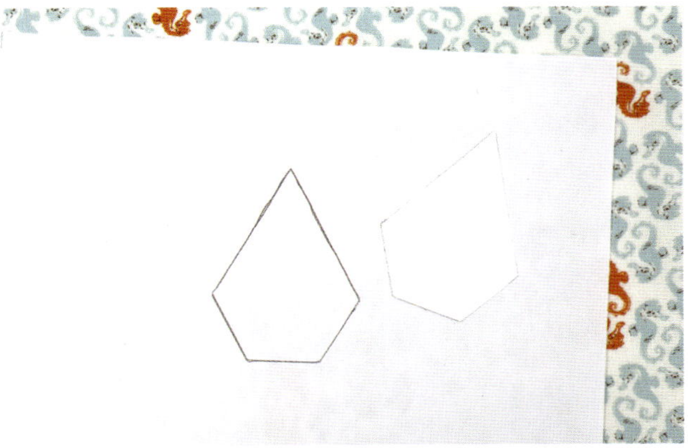

1. Place a jewel paper piece in the middle of the plain paper. Draw around the shape with a pencil.

2. Cut the shape out on the line with paper scissors. Lay the fabric right side up on a table or cutting mat. Place the paper on top of a design detail that you like. I use this as a viewing portal to preview the fabric before I commit to cutting.

3. Position the mirror on top of the paper, lining up the edges along the cutout. You will see the reflected image of the fabric through the paper cutout. If you are not happy with the motif you chose, just move the cutout and mirror around until you see something you like.

4. Look over the fabric to make sure that there are six usable repeats. Place the template over the paper cutout shape. Carefully slide the paper cutout out from under the template. With a marker, make a few guide (registration) marks on top of the template.

5. Using a pencil or fabric marking tool, draw a line around the template. Move the template to the next repeat, precisely matching the registration marks from the template. Repeat until you have traced six exactly matching sections of fabric. They are now ready to be cut out.

You can use this method with many different shapes. After a while, with practice, it will get easier to envision a design detail that would be good for fussy cutting.

Thread vs. Glue Basting

Thread Basting	Glue Basting
PROS	
Most common technique	Easier and faster
Papers pop out easily	More secure
CONS	
Less secure	Paper is harder to remove
Slower	Could leave sticky residue

Basting

There are two methods to basting EPP: thread basting and glue basting. Traditionally, thread basting was the only method done for EPP. The basting threads can be removed, and the papers pop out easily. In recent years, glue pens were designed, are readily available, and are easier to use. There is controversy about thread versus glue among the EPP community. Either method you use is fine, as long as you are happy with the results and enjoy the process. I will show you each method, and I encourage you to try both to see which one you are comfortable using and gives you the accurate results needed for precision fussy cutting.

When I began my journey in EPP, I used thread basting and found that the fabric wasn't secure enough around the papers that I needed for precision fussy cutting. So, I switched over to slim fabric glue pens, and I now only use glue basting for speed and accuracy. I can easily quadruple the amount of EPP I can baste with glue than with thread. I have found that for good fussy cutting, accuracy matters; with glue basting, I achieve better results.

THREAD BASTING

When thread basting, some stitchers like to baste the fabrics through the papers, but this only works with very thin papers. The basting is easily removed, and the papers pop out easily.

Use any thread material you like as long as the colors do not bleed onto the fabrics. Use a color similar to the fabric color if you plan on leaving the basting threads in.

FOR THIS PRACTICE LESSON, I WILL BE USING:

- Needle
- 50wt thread
- 1½" (3.8cm) hexagon paper piece
- Precut fabric, using the hexagon template
- Sewing pins (optional)
- Fabric glue stick (optional)
- Sewing clips
- Iron

1. Thread a slim needle with a knot, ready to use.

2. Place a paper template on the wrong side of the cutout fabric. You can place a straight pin in the center to hold the paper in place or tack it down with a dab of a glue stick.

3. Fold one side of the fabric seam allowance over the edge of the paper. Hold it in place with a clip. Turn the next seam allowance over the paper edge and finger press the fabric fold. Make a tacking stitch where the fabric overlaps in the corner. No need to sew through the paper.

4. Go to the next edge, turn the seam allowance over, and finger press. Make a tacking stitch where the fabric overlaps in the corner. Continue working all the corners until you meet up at the beginning, removing the pin or clip as you go. Press both sides with a hot iron.

Glue Basting Tips

- Hold the slim glue pen as you would an ink pen—at an angle. Do not glue with the flat top of the glue pen, just the edge.
- Only use a slight amount of glue; do not apply firm pressure.
- Apply glue to the paper, not the fabric seam allowance. Some glue will overlap onto the fabric, usually at the corners, and that's okay.
- If the glue gets gloppy from the warmth of your hand, put it into the refrigerator for about 30 minutes to firm up.

BASIC GLUE BASTING

By following a few guidelines, glue basting is fairly simple. I'll walk you through glue basting so with practice, you too can achieve excellent results.

FOR THIS PRACTICE LESSON, I WILL BE USING:

- Precut fabric, using the jewel template
- 1" (2.5cm) jewel paper piece
- Fabric glue stick
- Iron

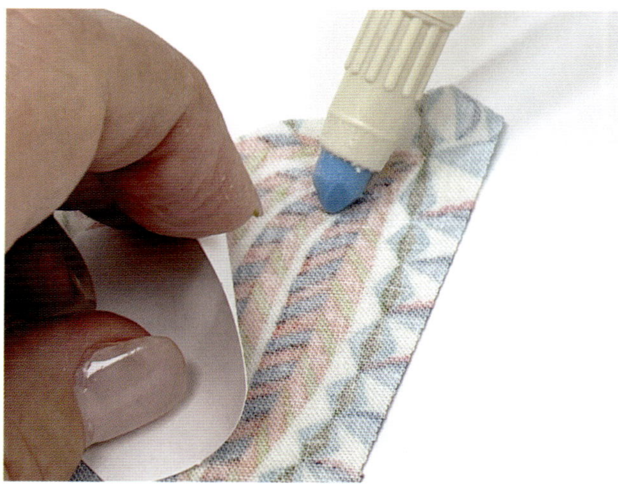

1. Lay the fabric piece right side down on the table. Center a paper piece on top, holding your finger on top of the paper so it doesn't move. Lift a corner of the paper and tap a dot of glue on top of the fabric. Do this in two places. This will hold the paper in place, but if you make a mistake, it is easy to reposition the paper.

2. Apply a thin line of glue away from the edge of the paper, so as not to interfere with the stitching and dulling the needle tip. Turn the seam allowance over with your finger and press to adhere.

3. Move over to the next edge and apply another line of glue, turn the seam allowance over and press. Continue around the entire piece. Give it a good press on both sides using a hot iron without steam or starch. Now it is ready to stitch to another EPP shape.

Tip

The correct way to hold the glue pen is similar to holding a pencil: at an angle. Now this is where I find many people make their mistakes in applying too much glue. You do not apply the glue with the flat top of the glue stick; only use the edge of the glue stick. All that is needed is a thin line of glue to adhere the seam allowance to the paper piece.

GLUE BASTING POINTS

Glue basting sharp points can be tricky, but with practice, it gets easier. I'll use a diamond for an example.

1. Place the precut fabric right side down and the paper piece on top. Tap a dot of glue between the fabric and paper at both ends to hold paper in position.

2. Apply a thin line of glue on the upper-left edge of paper and the opposite, bottom-right side. Turn seam allowance over and press to hold.

3. At the top point, fold the seam allowance back halfway and finger press. Apply a line of glue along the right top edge of the paper. Turn the seam allowance over and press to hold.

4. Rotate the diamond so the bottom point is now the top point. Repeat step 3.

5. Examine the points. You can use your fingernail to indent the crease for more definition. Press both sides with a hot iron.

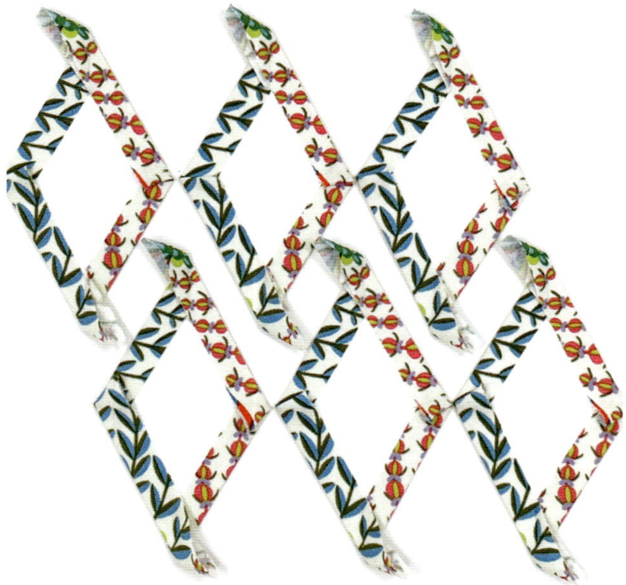

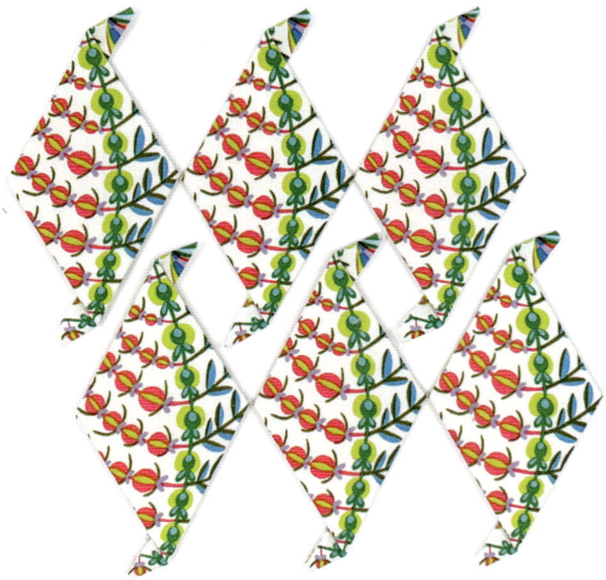

6. It is recommended to keep all the tails (flags, dog ears) going in the same direction, as it will become necessary when stitching them together. So don't cut them off!

GLUE BASTING FOR PRECISION FUSSY CUTTING

When you are glue basting for fussy cutting, you have to pay close attention to the exact alignment of the paper pieces on the fabric. This is a critical part of making kaleidoscope designs. I use this process whether I have four or twenty pieces to match up.

1. Lay the cutout fabrics on the table right side down. Place the paper shapes on top of the fabric pieces. The first one will be the master copy, which you will match the placement to as precisely as possible.

2. Place the paper exactly where you want it. Put your finger on top to keep it in place. Lift a corner of the paper and tap a dot of glue on the fabric.

3. Without lifting your finger, move over to another corner and lift the paper piece. Tap another dot of glue on the fabric. This will secure the paper piece from shifting and moving when you begin to glue baste the seam allowance.

4. Match up the remaining pieces to the master copy. Do one at a time by looking for any minute detail to use as a guide to line up and match the placement of the papers. I used pins here to mark all the points and corners.

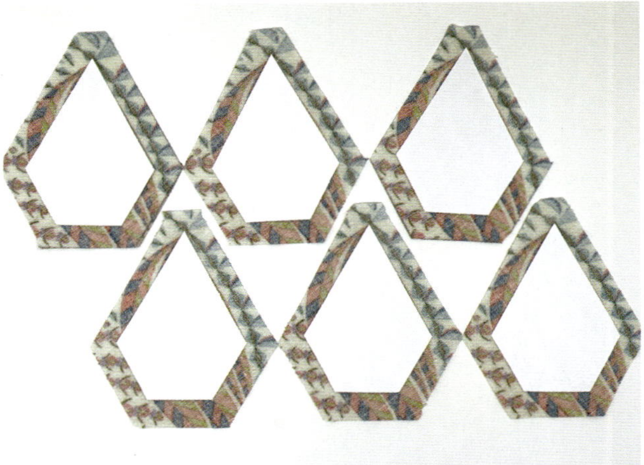

5. Secure the papers in the remaining pieces, as in step 2. When all the fabric pieces are done, you can glue baste the seam allowances. Press both sides with a hot iron.

Tip

After a few months working with EPP, I started pressing the pieces with a hot iron after I finished basting them. I found that it gave me a nice crisp edge of fabric to stitch on. My needle goes through the fabrics easier, and I didn't stitch through the paper edges as often. I encourage you to try it to see if it helps you also.

Stitching Techniques

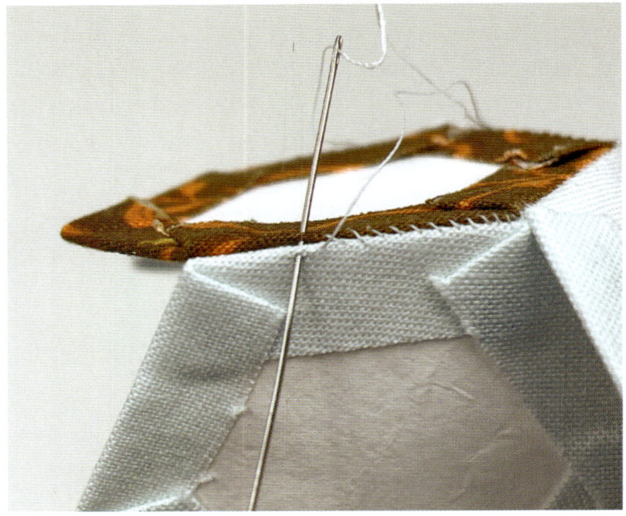

Whipstitch—The whipstitch is easy to do, and I use it primarily to join two prepared EPP shapes together.

1. Place two prepared pieces right sides together. Bury the knot in the corner by bringing the needle up from under the seam allowance.
2. Insert the needle into the folded edges of the paper pieces. About two to three threads on each edge are all that is needed. I call this "taking a small bite of the fabric."
3. Pass the needle and thread through the fabric, bring (whip) it around again, and insert it very closely to the last stitch you just made going in the same direction.

The standard number of stitches to use is 10 to 15 per 1" (2.5cm). If you feel the slightest resistance, you are hitting the edge of the papers inside; adjust the depth of where you inserted the needle. With practice, it gets easier to find just the right spot.

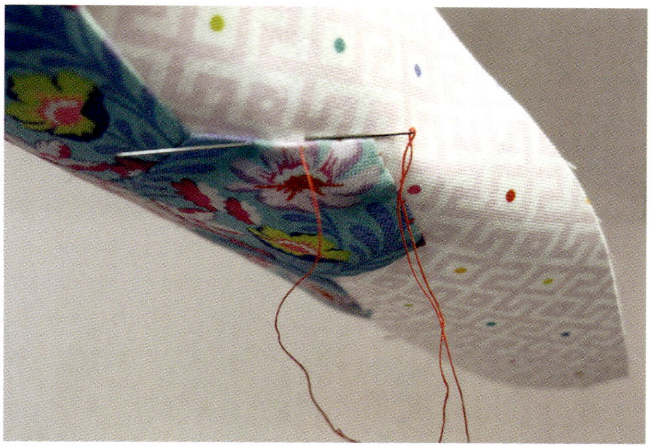

Blind (Ladder, Invisible, Slip) Stitch–This stitch is typically used in appliqué. I use this stitch when I appliqué an EPP block to the background fabric. The key is to keep the stitches parallel and directly across each piece, forming a "ladder" of stitching.

1. Bury the knot inside the fold of the first section. Bring the needle out of the fold and insert directly across into the fold of the section you are stitching together.
2. Bring the needle back out through the second fabric, parallel to the first stitch.
3. Insert the top of the needle into the fold of the first fabric. Bring the needle through.
4. Pull on the thread line to draw the seam/join together.

Twisted Knot–This is one that an adult likely taught you as a child. Twist the thread around your finger about two or three times, then roll it off. With a slight pull on the thread, it becomes a little knot. It can also become a larger nest of thread if you are not careful.

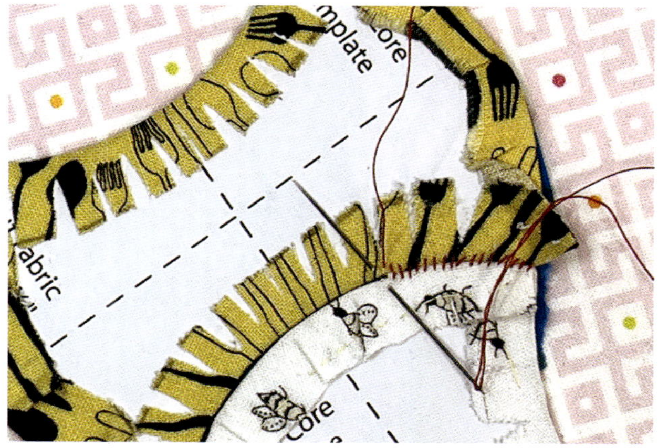

Flat-Back Stitch–This stitch is primarily used to join curved shapes, as in Apple Core and Scallops.

1. On a flat surface, place the prepared paper pieces with the right side up. Butt up the edges you wish to join. Place a piece of low-tack tape across to hold the pieces together. Turn the pieces over.
2. Starting at one end of the seam, bury the knot in the corner. With the needle and thread, make tiny stitches as you did with the whipstitch–only taking a tiny bite of fabric on each side of the seam edge.

Half-Hitch Knot–I make a half-hitch knot on every corner and valley while stitching my paper pieces together. I also make one when I end a seam. At the end of stitching, but before you pull the last stitch tight, there is a loop of thread. Pass the needle through the loop of thread, then pull it tight.

Ending a Seam—When I come to the end of the seam, I will make a half-hitch knot, then stitch back over the last two to three stitches using a whipstitch to secure.

Troubleshooting

For those new to English Paper Piecing, you might want to jump to the projects (starting on page 33) before reviewing these issues. You can then refer to this section when you encounter a problem. I typically run into a few problems while working on my EPP projects that need to be corrected. These remedies work well for me, and I encourage you to give them a try. I also encourage you to find something that would work for you.

Something doesn't look right. I'm not happy with my fabric choices or placement.

Take a picture of the block in color and in black and white. Sometimes seeing the design in a new way can make the problem stand out. Let it sit overnight, then see if it's still bothersome after some time has passed. If it is, make replacements by using different fabrics on new pieces. (I keep a baggie of surplus pieces that I have switched out from other blocks, saving them for other projects.) Place the new pieces on top of the existing ones and take another picture. If you like it, then go ahead and change them out.

I didn't like something about the left block. After making it black and white, I determined it was the center piece that was the issue. When I swapped it for the block on the right, this result was much more to my liking.

How do I replace pieces that I'm not happy with?
Locate the pieces that you want to replace. Using sharp, pointed scissors or a seam ripper, carefully snip the stitching thread, making sure not to snip the fabric. Many times, I will use a magnifying glass. I will work each seam by snipping the thread and gently pulling the pieces apart, opening up the seam to expose the thread.

I snip and pull, snip and pull, until the pieces come apart. When I'm done removing the pieces that I want replaced, I will clean up all the cut threads before I'm ready to rebuild my block. **Note:** If you should cut into the fabric, you will need to replace that piece as well, because it will inevitably unravel.

Once you find the sewing thread, carefully snip it.

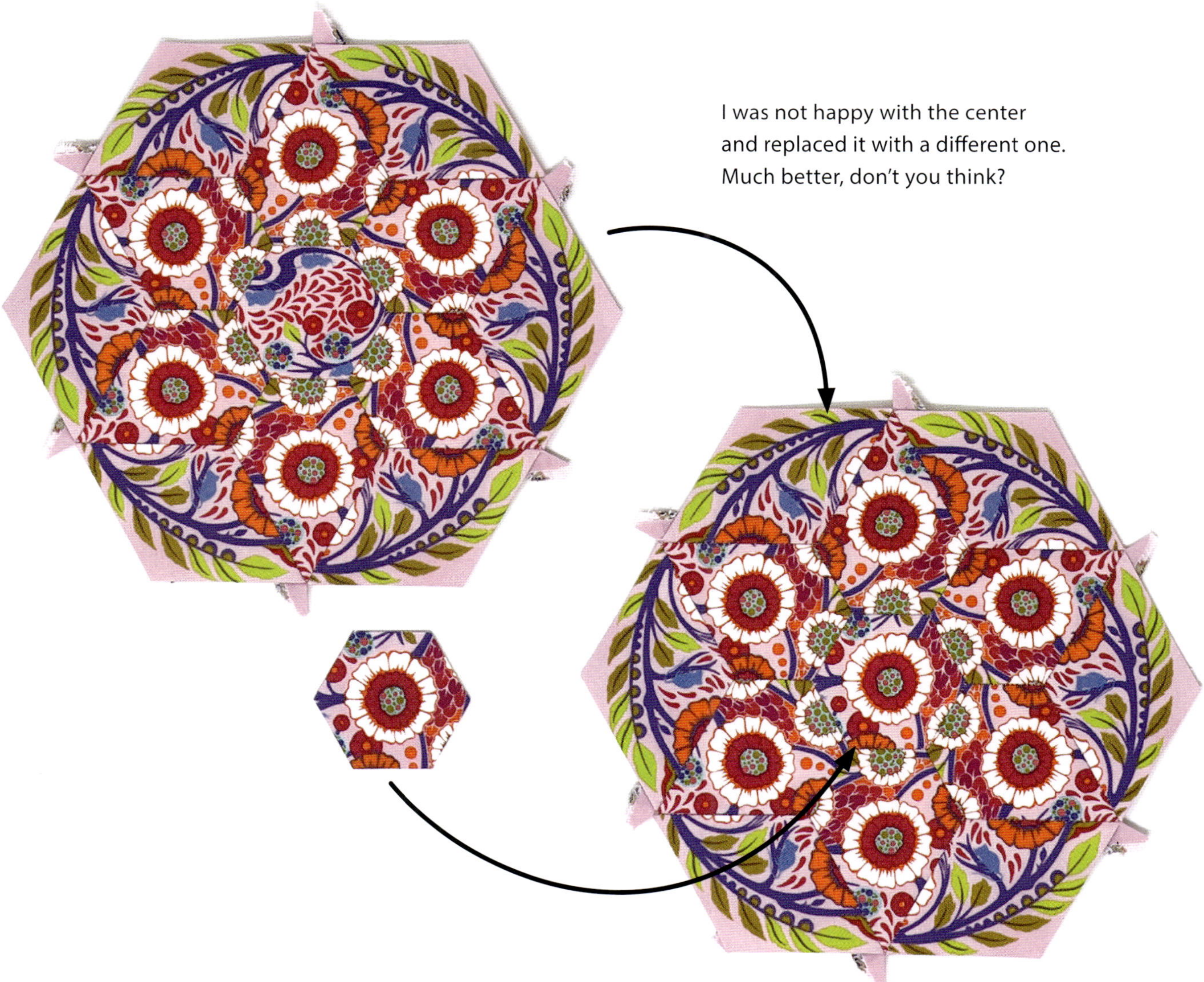

I was not happy with the center and replaced it with a different one. Much better, don't you think?

When stitching my pieces together, they are not matching up in length.

A technique I learned in sewing garments is called easing (to move or shift with care). With EPP, I start by matching up one corner, making three or four stitches, then knotting off. Go to the other corner and match it up (one piece will bow slightly in the center); clip it to hold in place. Begin stitching while putting slight pressure with your finger on the bowed-out center. As you stitch, distribute the stitches to the other end.

Sometimes when you hand cut out your paper pieces, they may not be exactly the same size.

Make sure to clip the pieces in place so they don't shift; plus, it takes the strain off your fingers.

I glue basted, and it's hard to remove the paper.

This usually happens when you are applying too much glue. Review the glue basting section (page 24). What tool are you using to remove the paper pieces? I have found that a Hera marker works best for me. Try warming the pieces with a dry iron. As a last resort, use a little water to moisten the glue and paper.

My stitching threads are showing on the front side.

For the best results, use quality thread that is thin but strong. I recommend 50 or 80wt. Match the thread color to the fabric and try taking smaller "bites" of the fabric.

When I'm done with my block, it does not lay flat.

When you are finished stitching your block, press it with a dry hot iron to hold its shape. After you have removed the papers, the fabrics will relax. Press it again, this time with fabric starch or a fine misting of water, before you appliqué it to a background. If you are making a large quilt, press it after all the blocks are sewn together.

I used both a green and red thread to stitch halfway along the edge of these pieces. The red blends in much better, whether looking from the back (top) or front (bottom).

Projects

Four projects—a pincushion, a pillow, and two quilts—are a perfect way to dip your toe into EPP and build your skills as you go. Let's get started.

Hexagon Pincushion

This simple project will get you familiar with the process of fussy cutting and EPP. Hexagons are the most familiar of paper pieces and used the most often. Using six hexagons surrounding a center hexagon is commonly called a hexie-flower or blossom. I will teach you how to navigate this simple shape along with fussy cutting to create a lovely pincushion.

Finished Size: 2" x 5½" x 5½" (5.1 x 14 x 14cm)
Skill Level: Beginner

SHAPES NEEDED

- (1) 1" (2.5cm) hexagon acrylic template
- (7) 1" (2.5cm) hexagon paper pieces

FABRIC NEEDED

Before cutting any fabrics, press to remove folds and wrinkles. Pressing after cutting will distort the small fabric pieces.

- Fat Quarter of focus fabric, or fabric scraps with at least six repeat designs
- (1) 7" x 7" (17.8 x 17.8cm) square for background
- (1) 7" x 7" (17.8 x 17.8cm) square for pincushion back

SUPPLIES NEEDED

- Iron
- Fabric scissors
- Hinged mirror
- Permanent marker
- Fabric marking tool
- Cotton pad and rubbing alcohol
- Fabric glue stick
- Needle and thread
- Thread conditioner
- Sewing clips
- Hera marker
- Starch spray
- Stuffing

INSTRUCTIONS

1. Play with the hinged mirror and hexagon template on the focus fabric. Find something interesting that you would like to fussy cut.

2. Fussy cut (see page 20) for a total of six hexagon shapes. Remove the marks from the template with a cotton pad and rubbing alcohol. Use the template to find something for the center hexagon and fussy cut it out.

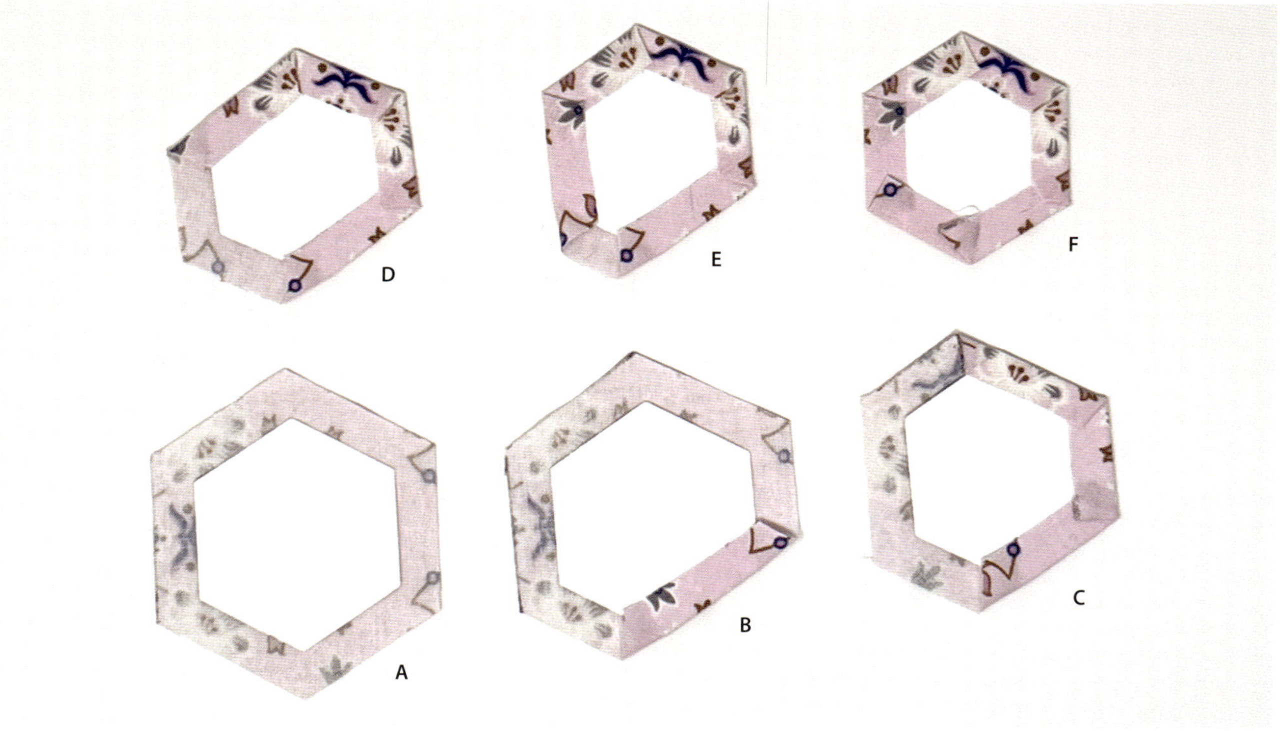

3. Following the Basic Glue Basting technique (page 24), baste the seam allowances (shown as A–F). Use the first one as the master copy and replicate on the remaining hexagons. If you make a mistake, it's easy enough to reposition the paper.

4. Lay out the hexagons in the way you want them stitched together. Prepare the needle and thread using thread conditioner. Join the outer hexagons around the center hexagon, in order and one at a time, using the whipstitch.

5. Stitch the side seams, starting at the outside edge and stitching toward the inside. Press it once more. You made your first hexie-flower!

6. Remove the paper pieces from inside each of the hexagons. Carefully pry up the basted fabric with a Hera marker or another tool of your choosing. Press all the seam allowances flat, using starch spray or a spritz of water to hold their shape. Press the front too.

7. Center the hexie-flower on top of the 7" x 7" (17.8 x 17.8cm) background fabric. Appliqué using the blind stitch.

8. Place the background fabric and 7" x 7" (17.8 x 17.8cm) pincushion back right sides together. Stitch using a ¼" (6.4mm) seam allowance. Leave a 2½" (6.4cm) opening along one side for turning.

9. Box corners by sewing on the diagonal ¾" (1.9cm) from the outside corners. Turn the fabric right side out. Press carefully. Stuff with fiberfill. Hand stitch the seam closed using a blind stitch. Finished!

These pincushions make a great gift, especially using orphaned hexie-flowers.

Jeweled Star Pillow

Take your EPP skills up to the next level by adding different piecing shapes and elements. With this next pattern, you will learn to work with different shapes and stitching order to make a unit, as if you are "putting the jigsaw pieces together." Using this technique, you could make larger pillows using orphaned blocks.

Finished Size: 12" x 12" (30.5 x 30.5cm)
Skill Level: Beginner

SHAPES NEEDED

- (1) 1" (2.5cm) hexagon acrylic template
- (1) 1" (2.5cm) hexagon paper piece
- (1) 1" (2.5cm) jewel acrylic template
- (6) 1" (2.5cm) jewel paper pieces
- (1) 2" (5.1cm) 60-degree diamond acrylic template
- (6) 2" (5.1cm) 60-degree diamond paper pieces

FABRIC NEEDED

Before cutting any fabrics, press to remove folds and wrinkles. Pressing after cutting will distort the small fabric pieces.

- Fat Quarter of focus fabric for fussy cutting
- Fat Quarter of contrast fabric for bias binding
- (1) 13" x 13" (33 x 33cm) square for background
- (1) 13" x 13" (33 x 33cm) batting
- (1) 13" x 13" (33 x 33cm) backing fabric
- (1) 13" x 16" (33 x 40.6cm) rectangle for pillow back

SUPPLIES NEEDED

- Iron
- Fabric scissors
- Hinged mirror
- Permanent marker
- Fabric marking tool
- Cotton pad and rubbing alcohol
- Fabric glue stick
- Needle and thread
- Thread conditioner
- Sewing clips
- Hera marker
- Starch spray
- (1) 14" (35.6cm) invisible zipper
- (1) 12" (30.5cm) pillow insert

INSTRUCTIONS

1. Play with the hinged mirror, jewel template, and diamond template on the focus fabric. Find something interesting for each template that you would like to fussy cut.

2. Fussy cut (see page 20) for a total of six jewel and six diamond shapes. Remove the marks from the template with a cotton pad and rubbing alcohol. Use the hexagon template to find something for the center and fussy cut it out.

Tip

Remember to wipe the template clean each time you use it with different prints.

3. Following the Glue Basting techniques (starting on page 24), baste the seam allowances. Use the first jewel and diamond as the master copies and replicate on the remaining jewel and diamond shapes. Remember to press both back and front.

4. Lay out the hexagon and jewels in the way you want them stitched together. Face the pointed end of the jewel outward. Prepare the needle and thread using thread conditioner. Join the outer jewels around the center hexagon, in order and one at a time, using the whipstitch.

5. Stitch the side seams on the jewels, starting at the outside edge and stitching toward the inside.

6. Stitch the diamonds between the valleys of the jewel pieces, working in the round. When done, press with a hot iron. Remove the paper pieces.

7. Appliqué the block to the 13" x 13" (33 x 33cm) background fabric by machine stitching or blind stitching by hand. Press the pillow top once more. Layer the 13" x 13" (33 x 33cm) backing fabric, 13" x 13" (33 x 33cm) batting, and pillow top, then baste all three together. Quilt as desired.

8. Make the pillow back, adding the zipper. **Note:** The fabric used in the following steps is for reference only.

8a. Cut a 3" x 13" (7.6 x 33cm) strip from the 13" x 16" (33 x 40.6cm) pillow back fabric. The larger rectangle will now measure 13" x 13" (33 x 33cm).

8b. On the upper edge of the 3" x 13" (7.6 x 33cm) strip, make a mark ½" (1.3cm) from the left side. Mark just above the top zipper stop on both sides of the zipper tape. Following invisible zipper instructions, position the left side of the zipper tape to the top edge of the 3" (7.6cm) strip so that marks align. Apply the zipper, stitching all the way to the left edge.

8c. Position the other half of the zipper to the bottom of the remaining rectangle as shown. Align the ½" (1.3cm) marks on the zipper and pillow back, and stitch again to apply the zipper all the way to the left edge.

8d. Close the zipper and trim off the excess zipper tape on the right side.

9. The back will be larger than the pillow front. Centering the EPP work, trim the pillow front to 12½" x 12½" (31.8 x 31.8cm). Place the pillow front and back wrong sides together, so the right sides are aligned (you've established a ½" [1.3cm] seam allowance on that side with the zipper insertion, so you don't want to trim that side) and the zipper opening on the back will finish at least 2" (5.1cm) from the bottom edge. Trim the pillow back in line with the pillow front.

10. Clip the pieces together and baste to secure. Make bias binding—I used two 2½" (6.4cm) x WOF strips—and bind the edges as you would on a quilt (see page 65). Stitch right through the end of the zipper slowly; backstitch here to create a zipper stop. Turn right side out, and carefully push out pillow cover corners. Insert the pillow form and you are done!

Alternative Blocks

Use these blocks as inspiration for how to make your own Jeweled Star Pillow. Despite using the same layout of hexagon, jewel, and diamond pieces, you can achieve very different results based on the fabric, color, and fussy cutting choices.

Aurora Quilt

When I began working with English paper piecing in 2016, I worked with the basic shapes of hexagons and honeycombs. As my skills grew, I became interested in designing my own patterns. Not being skilled with geometry and with my dyslexia difficulties, I found it was easier to draw and erase on graph paper until I had an image I thought would work for me. This was the Aurora EPP pattern; I've also provided one variation–essentially a different layout by adding one additional shape. My patterns give you a variety of options for you to use again and again.

Finished Quilt Size: 61" x 72" (154.9 x 182.9cm)
Finished Block Size: 12" x 12" (30.5 x 30.5cm)
Skill Level: Intermediate

SHAPES NEEDED

- (1) 1½" (3.8cm) 45-degree diamond acrylic template
- (240) 1½" (3.8cm) 45-degree diamond paper pieces
- (1) 4½" (11.4cm) shield acrylic template
- (240) 4½" (11.4cm) shield paper pieces
- (1) 2½" (6.4cm) 45-degree diamond acrylic template
- (240) 2½" (6.4cm) 45-degree diamond paper pieces
- (1) 3½" (8.9cm) 90-degree triangle acrylic template
- (120) 3½" (8.9cm) 90-degree triangle paper pieces

FABRIC NEEDED

Before cutting any fabrics, press to remove folds and wrinkles. Pressing after cutting will distort the small fabric pieces.

- Fabric scraps with at least eight repeat designs (see page 15 for amounts)
- Fabric scraps with a directional print (see page 15 for amounts)
- (2) 3¼" x 61" (8.3 x 154.9cm) border fabric
- (2) 3¼" x 66½" (8.3 x 168.9cm) border fabric
- (1) 71" x 82" (180.3 x 208.3cm) batting
- (1) 73" x 84" (185.4 x 213.4cm) backing fabric

SUPPLIES NEEDED

- Iron
- Fabric scissors
- Hinged mirror
- Permanent marker
- Fabric marking tool
- Cotton pad and rubbing alcohol
- Fabric glue stick
- Needle and thread
- Thread conditioner
- Sewing clips
- Hera marker
- Starch spray

INSTRUCTIONS

1. Fussy cut (see page 20) for a total of eight shield, eight 1½" (3.8cm) diamond, eight 2½" (6.4cm) diamond, and four triangle shapes. Following the Glue Basting Points technique (page 25), baste the seam allowances.

Tip

For the corner triangles, I used a directional print on the quilt. However, these stripes make it difficult to match points. Less experienced quilters could opt for a solid fabric or a sample of prints, as seen in step 8.

2. Lay out the 1½" (3.8cm) diamonds in the way you want them stitched together. Split into two groups of four diamonds. Prepare the needle and thread using thread conditioner. Stitch the sides for each group, in order and one at a time, using the whipstitch. Start at the outside edge and stitch toward the inside.

3. With right sides of the fabrics facing each other, stitch the two halves together. Match the center as precisely as you can. Most of the time, it's easier for me to start from one end, stitch to the center, and knot it off. Then I go to the other end and stitch to the center. Open the star and press with a dry hot iron.

Tip

When joining the EPP diamonds, I will make four or five stitches, then open the pair up to make sure the points meet. If they don't meet, make an adjustment or start over. Then continue stitching to the end. This is critical for having all eight points meet in the center.

4. On the back of the star, you will find the dog ears (flags). Make sure they overlap each other in the same direction to create a spiral. Press with a hot iron. This reduces the bulk at this intersection and allows the star to lie flat.

5. Stitch the shields between the valleys of the diamond pieces, working one at a time in the round. Stitch the side seams of the shields, starting at the outside edge and stitching toward the inside.

6. Stitch the 2½" (6.4cm) diamonds between the valleys of the shield pieces, working in the round. When done, press with a hot iron. The Aurora block is complete. If desired, you can simply appliqué the block to a background fabric.

7. Stitch the triangle pieces to the corners. Press with an iron and remove the paper pieces.

8. Repeat on as many blocks as desired. For my quilt, I created 30 Aurora blocks and arranged them in six rows of five blocks.

Tip

As you build your quilt, it can be quite bulky and cumbersome to stitch. By removing the inner papers only, it is easier to get your hands around the blocks to connect them. It's important to leave the outer papers that surround your project in until you're completely finished.

9. Before stitching anything together, lay the finished blocks out on the floor in a way that is pleasing. Take a picture to remember the placement of each block.

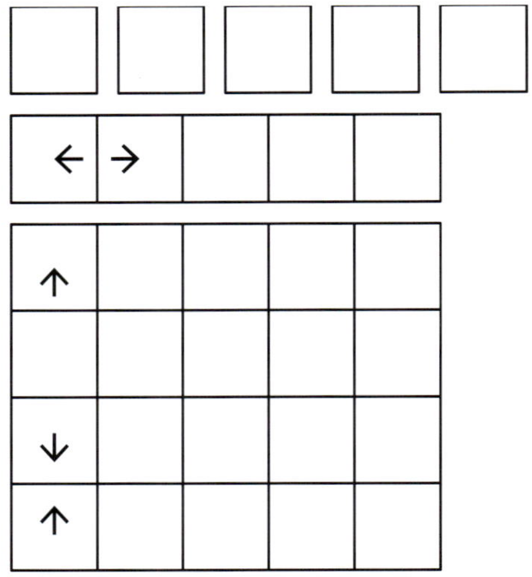

10. Join the blocks in each row; press seam allowances open between blocks. Join the rows; press seam allowances in opposite directions from row to row (up Row 2, down Row 2, etc.).

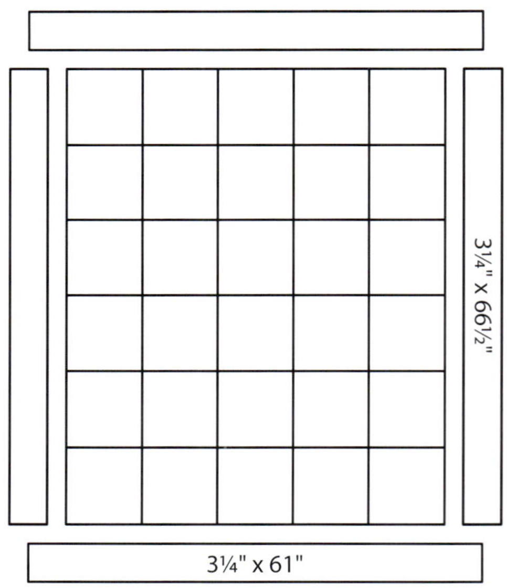

11. Add 3¼" x 61" (8.3 x 154.9cm) side borders, and press seams away from the quilt center. Add 3¼" x 66½" (8.3 x 168.9cm) top and bottom borders, and press seams away from the quilt center.

12. Layer with batting and backing. Quilt and bind as desired. See the Finishing section (page 64) for more instructions.

Aurora Quilt Variation

SHAPES NEEDED

- (1) 1½" (3.8cm) 45-degree diamond acrylic template
- (200) 1½" (3.8cm) 45-degree diamond paper pieces
- (1) 4½" (11.4cm) shield acrylic template
- (200) 4½" (11.4cm) shield paper pieces
- (1) 2½" (6.4cm) 45-degree diamond acrylic template
- (160) 2½" (6.4cm) 45-degree diamond paper pieces
- (1) 3¼" (8.3cm) kite acrylic template
- (64) 3¼" (8.3cm) kite paper pieces

FABRIC NEEDED

Before cutting any fabrics, press to remove folds and wrinkles. Pressing after cutting will distort the small fabric pieces.

- Fabric scraps with at least eight repeat designs (see page 15 for amounts)
- Solid black fabric (see page 15 for amounts)
- Fabric scraps with a directional print (see page 15 for amounts)

SUPPLIES NEEDED

- Iron
- Fabric scissors
- Hinged mirror
- Permanent marker
- Fabric marking tool
- Cotton pad and rubbing alcohol
- Fabric glue stick
- Needle and thread
- Thread conditioner
- Sewing clips
- Hera marker
- Starch spray

1. Fussy cut and baste the eight shield and eight 1½" (3.8cm) diamond shapes. Sew together as in steps 2–5 of the Aurora block. Repeat to make as many blocks as desired. Lay them out in an order that appeals to you. Take a picture for reference.

2. With solid black fabric, cut and baste 2½" (6.4cm) diamonds. Join one to the bottom shield pieces as in step 6 of the Aurora block. Make rows by connecting the blocks; nest the diamond from one block into the next, and stitch into place.

3. Make the row as long as you like, making as many rows as you like. The example quilt is five rows of five blocks.

4. With a directional print fabric, fussy cut and baste four kite pieces. Stitch together to form a cross.

5. Stitch four 2½" (6.4cm) diamonds to the cross.

6. Stitch the crosses in between the joined blocks.

7. Stitch 2½" (6.4cm) diamonds to the blocks in the spaces above and below the crosses.

8. Join another prepared row to the previous row. Nest them together and stitch into place.

9. Repeat until all rows, crosses, and diamonds are connected. Join the remaining 2½" (6.4cm) diamonds to the blocks on the outer edges. Refer to the tip box on page 50 about removing paper pieces. Appliqué to a piece of background fabric for your quilt top.

Sarafina Quilt

While working on one of my Aurora quilts, my mind wandered, as it so frequently does, to developing this new pattern. The Sarafina EPP pattern also has two versions. In the original design, the center has the eight-point star as in the Aurora pattern. The second version has a large center octagon to showcase a larger fabric design. I devised a method of making a large, circled frame to stitch the block too, which serves as an alternative to needle-turn appliqué. You can build your skills as you make this kaleidoscope.

Finished Size: 64" x 64" (162.6 x 162.6cm)
Finished Block Size: 14½" x 14½" (36.8 x 36.8cm)
Skill Level: Advanced

SHAPES NEEDED

- (1) 1½" (3.8cm) 45-degree diamond acrylic template
- (104) 1½" (3.8cm) 45-degree diamond paper pieces
- (1) 1½" (3.8cm) square acrylic template
- (104) 1½" (3.8cm) square paper pieces
- (1) 4" (10.2cm) kite acrylic template
- (72) 4" (10.2cm) kite paper pieces
- (1) 3" (7.6cm) kite acrylic template
- (72) 3" (7.6cm) kite paper pieces
- (1) 2½" (6.4cm) curved-edge triangle acrylic template
- (144) 2½" (6.4cm) curved-edge triangle paper pieces
- (1) 7" (17.8cm) frame corner acrylic template
- (36) 7" (17.8cm) frame corner paper pieces

FABRIC NEEDED

Before cutting any fabrics, press to remove folds and wrinkles. Pressing after cutting will distort the small fabric pieces.

- Fabric scraps with at least eight repeat designs (see page 15 for amounts)
- Fabric scraps with a directional print (see page 15 for amounts)
- 1½ yards (1.4m) background fabric
- (2) 1¼" x 44" (3.2 x 111.8cm) border 1 fabric
- (2) 1¼" x 45½" (3.2 x 115.6cm) border 1 fabric
- (396) 2" x 2" (5.1 x 5.1cm) assorted squares for border 2
- (2) 1¼" x 54½" (3.2 x 138.4cm) border 3 fabric
- (2) 1¼" x 56" (3.2 x 142.2cm) border 3 fabric
- (2) 4¼" x 56" (10.8 x 142.2cm) border 4 fabric
- (2) 4¼" x 64" (10.8 x 162.6cm) border 4 fabric
- (1) 74" x 74" (188 x 188cm) batting
- (1) 76" x 76" (193 x 193cm) backing fabric

SUPPLIES NEEDED

- Iron
- Fabric scissors
- Hinged mirror
- Permanent marker
- Fabric marking tool
- Cotton pad and rubbing alcohol
- Fabric glue stick
- Needle and thread
- Thread conditioner
- Sewing clips
- Hera marker
- Starch spray
- Sewing pins
- Liquid glue for basting

MAKING THE SARAFINA BLOCK

1. Fussy cut (see page 20) for a total of eight diamond and eight 4" (10.2cm) kite shapes. With directional print fabrics, fussy cut eight square, eight 3" (7.6cm) kite, and sixteen curved-edge triangle shapes. Following the Glue Basting techniques (starting on page 24), baste the seam allowances.

2. Lay out the diamonds in the way you want them stitched together. Split into two groups of four. Stitch the sides for each group, in order and one at a time, using the whipstitch. Start at the outside edge and stitch toward the inside. With right sides of the fabrics facing each other, stitch the two halves together. Open the star and press with a hot iron.

3. Stitch the squares between the valleys of the diamond pieces, working in the round. Stitch the 4" (10.2cm) kites between the valleys of the square pieces, working in the round.

4. Make a subsection. Stitch a curved-edge triangle on either side of one 3" (7.6cm) kite. Repeat for a total of eight subsections.

5. Stitch the subsections between the valleys of the 4" (10.2cm) kite pieces, working in the round. When done, press with a hot iron.

6. Remove the paper pieces from inside each shape. Press the front and back flat, including the outer edge, using starch spray.

7. The Sarafina block is complete. If desired, you can appliqué it to the background fabric, completing the quilt block (proceed to step 20).

MAKING THE FRAME

8. Cut four frame corner shapes from the background fabric. Make sure to allow for a generous seam allowance, ½" (1.3cm) along the inner curve. **Note:** For making a pillow with a wider background, increase the two outside corner seam allowance up to 1½" (3.8cm).

9. Glue baste the two long edges and the two short edges to the paper templates. Along the curved edge, use the tips of sharp scissors to snip the fabric about ½" (1.3cm) apart. Be careful not to snip too deep.

10. Run a short line of glue close to the edge of the curve. Flip over the seam allowance and finger press. Continue to the end.

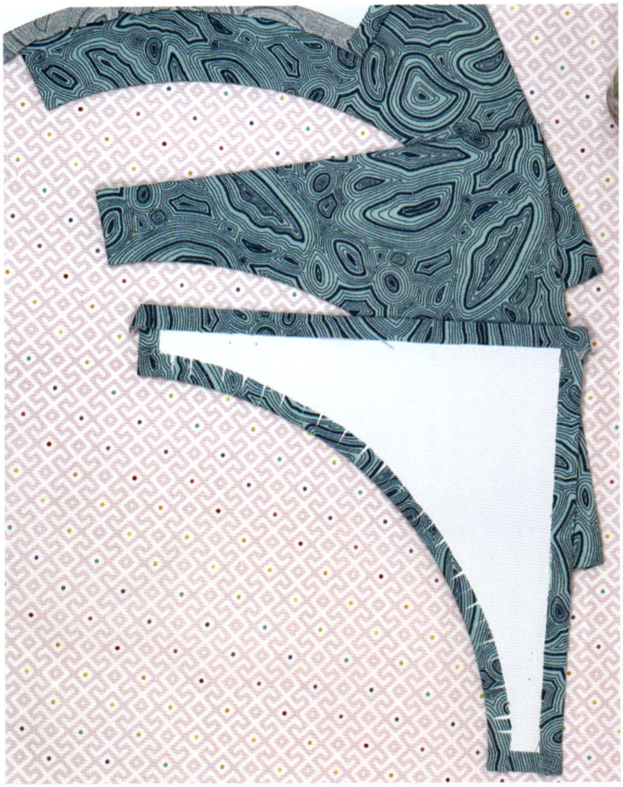

11. Press with a hot dry iron on all five edges to get nice, crisp fabric edges to stitch on. Repeat with the three other corner pieces.

12. With right sides up, line up the four frame corner pieces in the way you want them stitched together. This will form a circle. Stitch the short ends together to join.

ASSEMBLING THE QUILT BLOCK

13. Move the Sarafina block to an ironing board and position where you want the top and bottom to be. Position and center the frame on top. The connected edges of the frame should line up with the 4" (10.2cm) kite points. Stick pins through the frame pieces into the ironing board to hold it in place.

14. Working one frame piece at a time, remove the pins and lift the outside corner. Apply a thin line of basting glue along the curved edge of the paper template, right over the seam allowance. Do not add glue to the Sarafina block.

15. Lower the frame over the Sarafina block. Using the hot iron, press it carefully for about three to five seconds. Repeat on all four corners.

16. Once it's cooled down, you may lift the quilt block from the ironing board. It will hold while you stitch.

STITCHING THE QUILT BLOCK

17. Using the blind stitch, stitch along the curve with a thread color that matches the fabric of the circle frame. Stitch all the way around.

18. Remove the paper pieces from inside each of the frame corners. Trim and tidy up the seam allowance.

19. With right side up, press with a hot iron to set the circle seam. Machine stitch very close to the edge, about 1⁄16" (1.6mm), to reinforce it.

MAKING THE ROSETTE BLOCK

20. Fussy cut for a total of eight diamond and eight square shapes. Following the Glue Basting techniques, baste the seam allowances.

21. Lay out the diamonds in the way you want them stitched together. Split into two groups of four. Stitch the sides for each group using the whip stitch. With right sides facing, stitch the two halves together. Open the star and press with a hot iron.

22. Stitch the squares between the valleys of the diamond pieces, working in the round.

ASSEMBLING THE QUILT

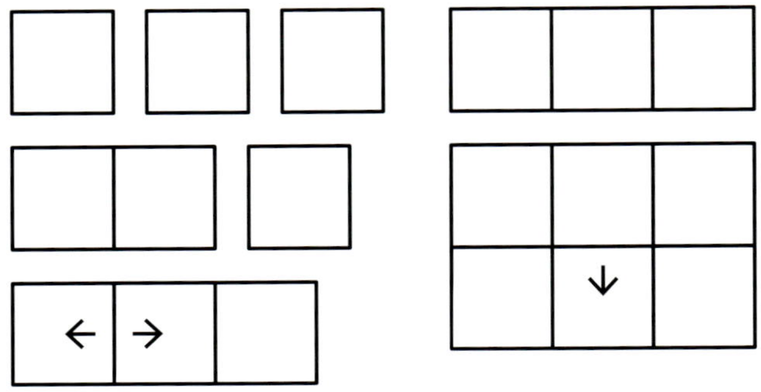

23. Create nine Quilt blocks and arrange in three rows of three blocks. Join the blocks in each row, then join the rows. Press seam allowances in alternating directions from row to row.

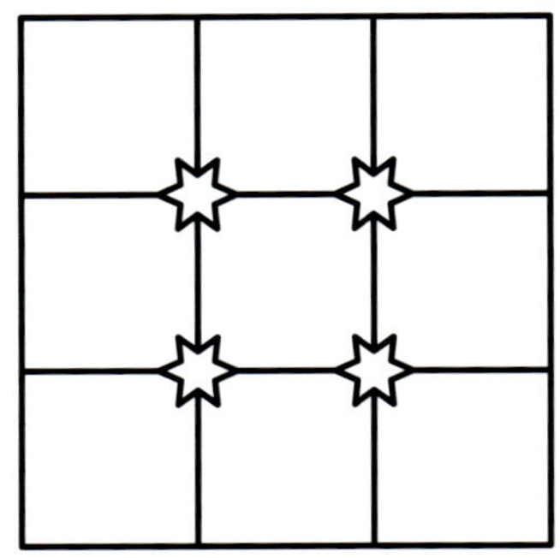

24. Create four Rosette blocks. Align the valleys with the connected edges of the Quilt blocks. Appliqué to the four intersections of the Quilt blocks, turning under 1⁄4" (6.4mm) seam allowances and using a blind stitch.

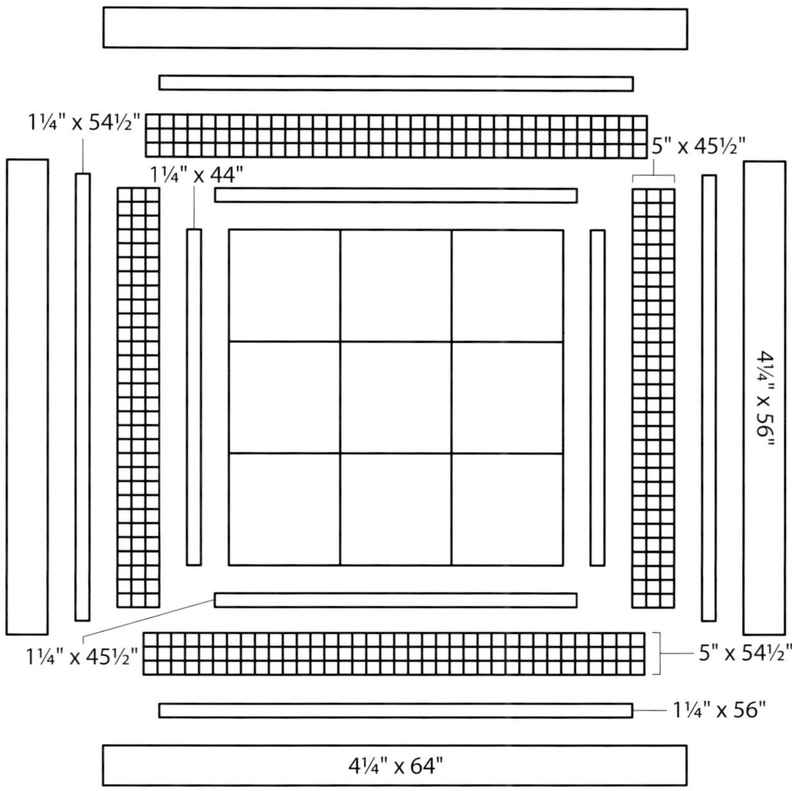

25. Add 1¼" x 44" (3.2 x 111.8cm) side borders, and press seams away from the quilt center. Add 1¼" x 45½" (3.2 x 115.6cm) top and bottom borders, and press seams away from the quilt center.

26. Arrange and join 2" x 2" (5.1 x 5.1cm) squares into three rows of 30 squares to create a pieced 5" x 45½" (12.7 x 115.6cm) side border unit. Repeat for a second pieced unit. Add units to sides of quilt center. Press seams toward the pieced border.

27. Arrange and join 2" x 2" (5.1 x 5.1cm) squares into three rows of 36 squares to create a pieced 5" x 54½" (12.7 x 138.4cm) top border unit. Repeat for a bottom pieced unit. Add units to top and bottom of quilt center. Press seams toward the pieced border.

28. Add 1¼" x 54½" (3.2 x 138.4cm) side borders, and press seams toward the quilt center. Add 1¼" x 56" (3.2 x 142.2cm) top and bottom borders, and press seams toward the quilt center.

29. Add 4¼" x 56" (10.8 x 142.2cm) side borders, and press seams away from the quilt center. Add 4¼" x 64" (10.8 x 162.6cm) top and bottom borders, and press seams away from the quilt center.

30. Layer with batting and backing. Quilt and bind as desired. See the Finishing section (page 64) for more instructions.

Sarafina Block Variation

I made this variation to utilize larger designs or to highlight a special motif. The instructions will be for constructing one block. You can make as many blocks that you may need for your project.

SHAPES NEEDED

- (1) 2⅛" (5.4cm) octagon acrylic template
- (1) 2⅛" (5.4cm) octagon paper piece
- (1) 1½" (3.8cm) 90-degree triangle acrylic template
- (8) 1½" (3.8cm) 90-degree triangle paper pieces
- (1) 4" (10.2cm) kite acrylic template
- (8) 4" (10.2cm) kite paper pieces
- (1) 3" (7.6cm) kite acrylic template
- (8) 3" (7.6cm) kite paper pieces
- (1) 2½" (6.4cm) curved-edge triangle acrylic template
- (16) 2½" (6.4cm) curved-edge triangle paper pieces
- (1) 7" (17.8cm) frame corner acrylic template
- (4) 7" (17.8cm) frame corner paper pieces

FABRIC NEEDED

Before cutting any fabrics, press to remove folds and wrinkles. Pressing after cutting will distort the small fabric pieces.

- Fabric scraps with at least eight repeat designs (see page 15 for amounts)
- (1) 18" x 22" (30.5 x 55.9cm) background fabric

SUPPLIES NEEDED

- Iron
- Fabric scissors
- Hinged mirror
- Permanent marker
- Fabric marking tool
- Cotton pad and rubbing alcohol
- Fabric glue stick
- Needle and thread
- Thread conditioner
- Sewing clips
- Hera marker
- Starch spray
- Sewing pins
- Basting glue

1. Fussy cut (see page 20) for a total of eight triangle, eight 4" (10.2cm) kite, eight 3" (7.6cm) kite, and sixteen curved-edge triangle shapes. Use the octagon template to find something for the center and fussy cut it out. Following the Glue Basting techniques (starting on page 24), baste the seam allowances.

2. Lay out the octagon and triangles in the way you want them stitched together. Stitch the triangles on the edges of the octagon piece, working in the round.

3. Join the 4" (10.2cm) kite, 3" (7.6cm) kite, curved-edge triangle, and frame shapes as in steps 3–19 of the Sarafina block.

Finishing

Now that the meticulous handwork is done, I hope you give as much care and consideration to the back and binding for the overall appearance of your artwork. It most likely will become a heirloom to be loved and cherished for years to come.

Backizng

Backing can be approached in a couple different ways. By far, the simplest option is to purchase a single cut of backing or quilt fabric. For smaller projects, standard yardage (44" [1.1m]) may suffice as long as that width is at least 5" (12.7cm) larger than your quilt top all around. Yardage manufactured as quilt backing comes in widths from 104"–120" (2.6–3m), which is great if you're making one pretty large quilt or more than one quilt that works with the same fabric.

What is more common is to piece panels of standard quilting yardage—two or three panels cut the same length and joined horizontally or vertically. It is recommended to use horizontal seams for quilts 60" (1.5m) and smaller, and vertical seams for larger quilts.

Quilt Sandwich

To prepare for quilting and securing the layers, you need to create a quilt sandwich. Place the backing wrong side up, lay the batting on top of the backing, and place the quilt top wrong side down on top of the batting. Smooth the layers. The batting and the backing should always be 5"–6" (12.7–15.2cm) larger than the quilt top all around, as these elements tend to draw up during the quilting process. Once quilted, you trim the excess batting and backing in line with the quilt top.

If quilting on a sewing machine or by hand, the layers need to be pinned sufficiently with quilt pins—placed every 2"–3" (5.1–7.6cm)—or basted to keep the layers from shifting during the quilting

From left to right: quilt top, batting, and backing fabric. This is the same order that you should layer all your quilts.

process. Larger projects or more intricate quilting designs are better taken to a professional long arm service. This process of stitching patterns into your quilt sandwich requires special tools and skillsets. Smaller projects can be finished on a home machine using free-motion techniques. Very simple quilting can be done by following the seam lines (called stitch-in-the-ditch quilting).

Binding

The tutorial here shows a double-fold binding, which starts with 2½" (6.4cm) wide strips. Strips are cut from the width of fabric (WOF), which is generally 44" (111.8cm) wide. If, for example, you need 175" (444.5cm) of binding. To determine the binding length for your quilt, these are the calculations you'll need:

- Measure the quilt length and width, multiply by two, and add 10" (25.4cm).
- Since standard quilting cotton is 42"–45" (106.7–114.3cm) wide, estimate the useable fabric width (minus the selvages) at 40" (101.6m).
- The most common binding strips are 2¼"–2½" (5.7–6.3cm) wide.

Assuming the quilt is 36" x 60" (91.4 x 152.4cm), follow these steps:

1. Double the width to 72" (182.9cm) and the length to 120" (304.8cm).
2. Add together: 72 + 120 =192 (182.9 + 304.8 = 487.7).
3. Add 10" (25.4cm) for a total of 202" (513.1cm) of binding.
4. Divide 202" (513.1cm) by 40" (101.6m)—which is fabric width—to determine the number of strips needed; in this case, it's 5.05.
5. Always round up, so you'll want to cut 6 strips.

Just know that you will lose approximately 3" (7.6cm) in length with each join, so make sure to cut enough strips; too long is always better than being too short.

JOINING BINDING ENDS

To join binding strips smoothly and avoid a lump along the edge of the quilt or project, it is best to join the strips with an angled seam rather than just placing right sides together and stitching a straight seam from edge to edge.

1. Join binding strips by overlapping, right sides together, the end of one strip perpendicular with the end of a second strip; you should have a L shape. Draw a diagonal line from the upper outer edge of the top strip to the lower outer edge of the bottom strip.

2. Stitch a diagonal seam directly on top of the guideline. Trim with a pinking sheer for a ¼" (6.4mm) seam allowance. Press the seam allowance open.

3. Fold the binding strip in half lengthwise, wrong sides facing, and press. With raw edges aligned, pin the binding strip to the edge of the quilt and secure with pins or quilt clips. Leave at least 5" (12.7cm) of unstitched binding as a tail.

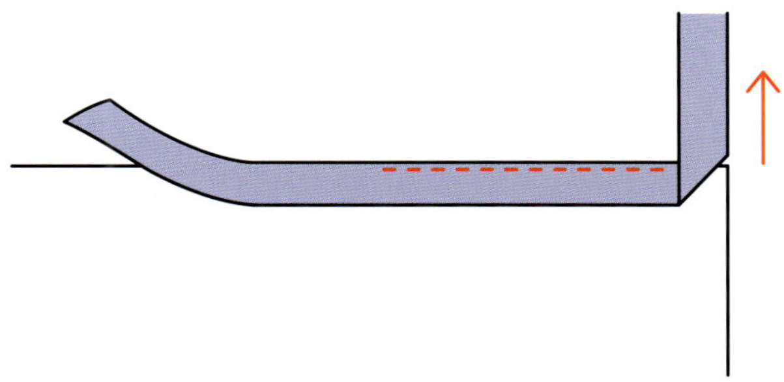

4. Stitch the binding to the quilt (sample uses a ½" [1.3cm] seam allowance), and as you approach the corner, stop stitching ½" (1.3cm) before you reach the edge. Secure the stitching using a backstitch. Fold the binding up at a 90-degree angle.

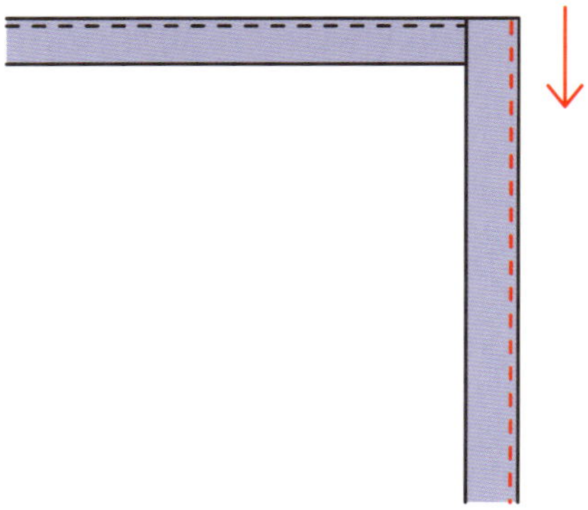

5. Fold the binding back down so the raw edge of the binding is flush with the raw edge of the quilt and the top fold is aligned with the original side. Stitch down the next side, making sure to fix the stitch line at the starting point. The binding will cup around the corner naturally with this technique.

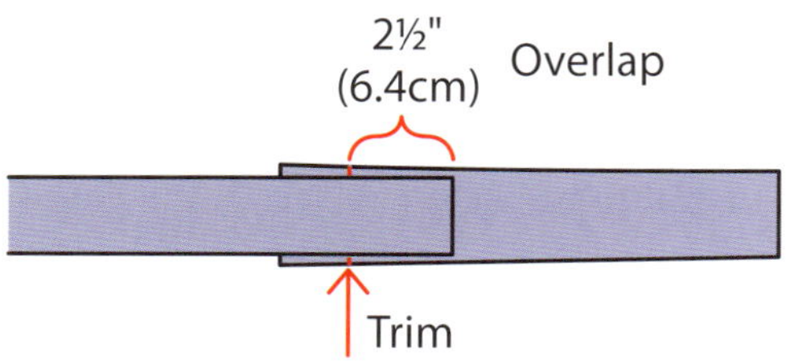

6. Continue around the quilt, stopping approximately 5"–6" (12.7–15.2cm) from the starting point. Place the tails smooth and flat along the edge. The overlap needs to be the same amount as the width of the binding (a 2½" [6.4cm] binding means a 2½" [6.4cm] overlap). Cut off the excess ends perpendicular to the edge of the quilt.

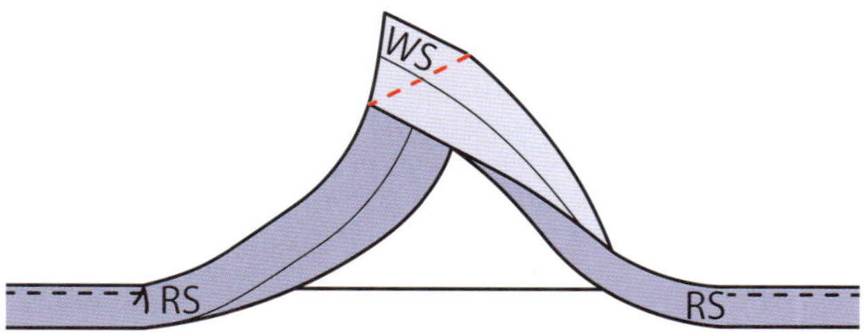

7. Place the cut ends right sides together at right angles, as you did to join the binding strips. Pin to secure and stitch a diagonal line from corner to corner and trim off the corner, leaving a ¼" (6mm) seam allowance.

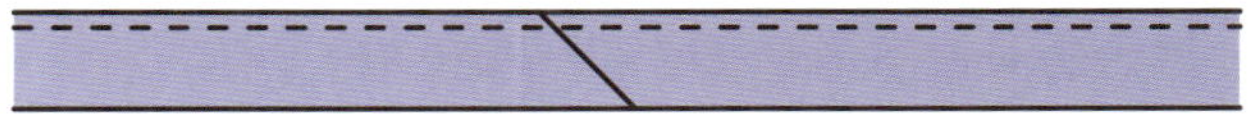

8. Finger press the binding into its original folded shape along the remaining raw edge of the quilt. Press, pin, and continue stitching, securing the stitch line as you start and stop.

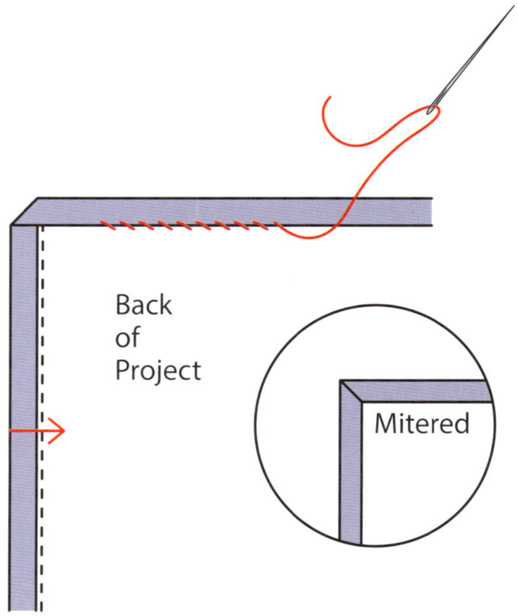

9. Press the binding away from the front edge and fold it over to the back of the quilt. Miter the binding at the corner and hand stitch into place with a single thread, a whipstitch or blind stitch.

Templates

Copy the page and cut the template out. This way, you can copy as many as you like.

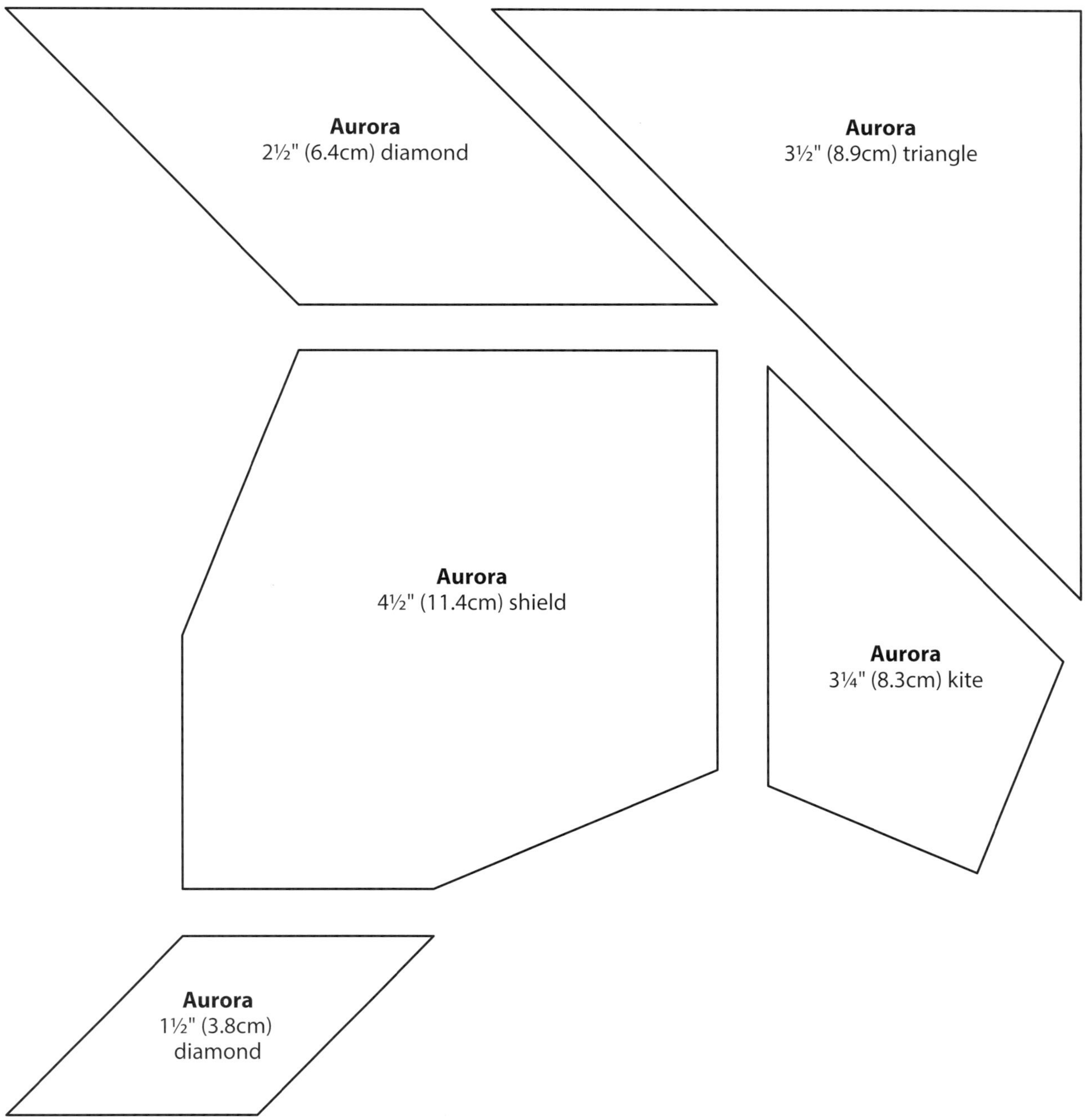

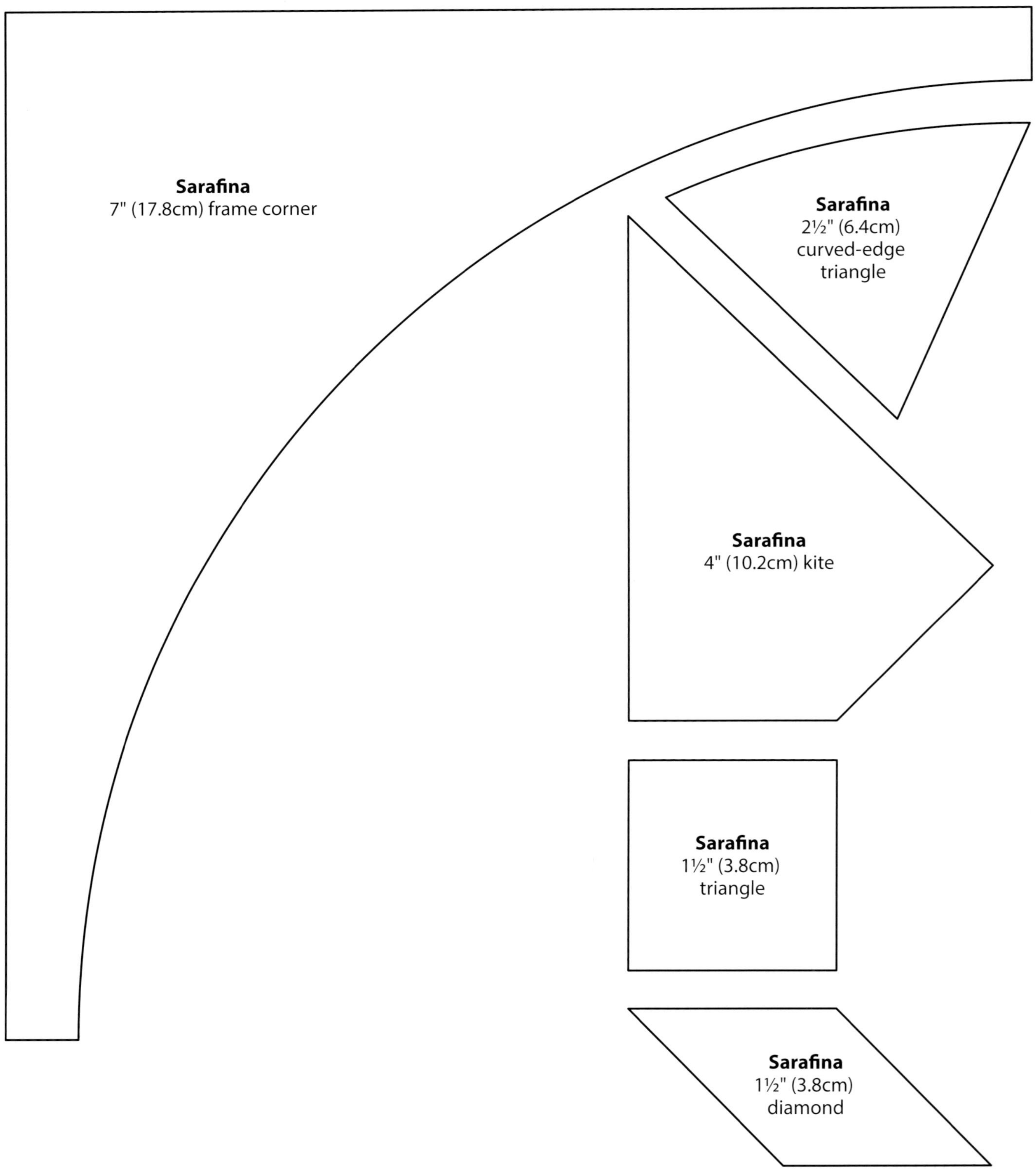
Sarafina
7" (17.8cm) frame corner
Sarafina
2½" (6.4cm)
curved-edge
triangle
Sarafina
4" (10.2cm) kite
Sarafina
1½" (3.8cm)
triangle
Sarafina
1½" (3.8cm)
diamond

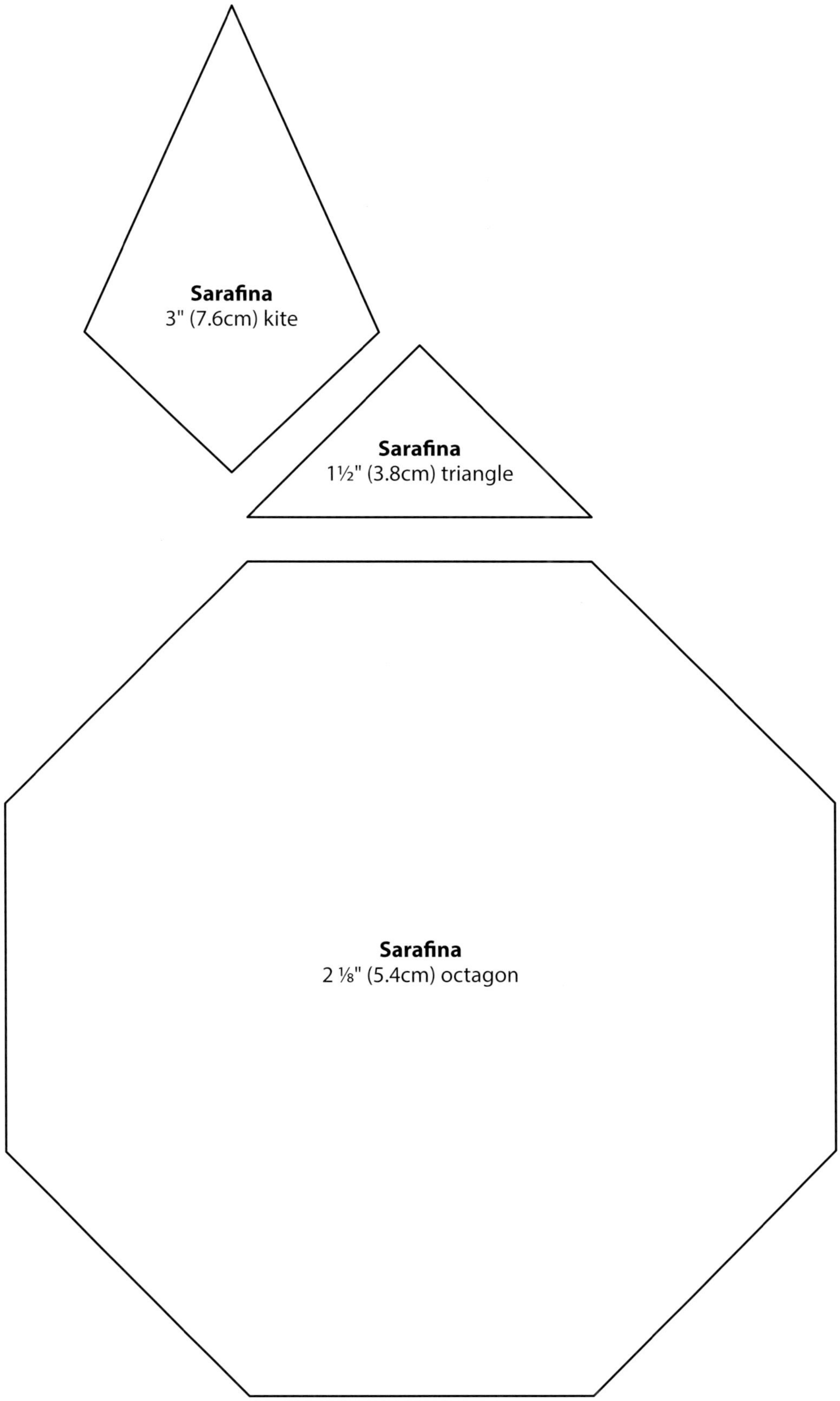
Sarafina
3" (7.6cm) kite
Sarafina
1½" (3.8cm) triangle
Sarafina
2 ⅛" (5.4cm) octagon

About the Author

Lydia Cheney is a long-time sewist, quilter, knitter, crafter, and teacher. Her EPP blocks garnered thousands of views online, but she has yet to make any of them available in pattern form for consumers. Having immigrated from Austria at a very young age, she's an artist influenced by her Austrian mother and Ukrainian father with an appreciation for traditional handcrafted clothing and the surroundings of those cultures.

Her journey into needlework started at age 11 when her sister taught her to knit, which led to a lifelong exploration into handcrafts. During home economics in junior high school, she started learning the basics of sewing and various needlework. As an adult, she learned that she had dyslexia and quicky realized how much she struggled with constant mistakes in reading instructions and measuring traditional patchwork. She also realized that the many crafts that she endeavored to accomplish she had to teach herself through trial and error. At that point, she realized that she was creating designs by using different approaches to figure things out. Even with her struggles with dyslexia, she relied on her intuitive nature and took advantage of being very visual, discovering she had the ability to create original designs.

In this, her first book, she will introduce the quilting community to her process; break it down so quilters can create beautiful, handcrafted items and quilts; and help others fall in love with the art of EPP.

Acknowledgments

First of all, this book would not be possible without the invaluable assistance and guidance from Amelia Johanson and Christa Oestreich and the team at Fox Chapel Publishing. They've shown me an abundance of encouragement and patience when working with me, and I know it wasn't easy at times. Thank you for making this book become a reality.

I have loved Teresa Silva's mastery of long arm quilting for a long time. She gives my quilts that special touch to accentuate the designs like icing on a cake. Thank you. Your workmanship is beautiful.

To my daughter Michelle, for her skills and talents as a graphic artist and tech support. Your help was immeasurable with your generous heart and willingness to help your mom out.

To my niece Roxanne, for taking the time to help me with photos and tech support—you're the sweetest. For my loving family for their encouragement and support.

I could not leave out my psychiatrist, Dr. Anna Lembke, for giving me my life back and for the many years working with me to recover from PTSD and several traumas. It was a difficult time in my life, but you helped to make sense out of it and helped me heal and move forward. I would not have been able to do what I do today without her guidance. She has shown me that quilting and creating are very much a part of therapy.

To Sandy Liou, my therapist, who sat and listened to me once a week while I talked my way through the process of writing this book. Thank you for making sense of my insecurities and believing in me.

A special thank-you to all the wonderful fabric designers who provide amazing, diverse fabrics I get to cut up and play with. There is such an abundance of fabrics to choose from with new ones in the works. There's just not enough time to make all the things I dream of.

Thank you to all the stitchers and new friends I've made from Instagram and Facebook groups. For their encouragement, funnies, shared creative support, and commiseration over current affairs. Viewing all the posts of their beautiful works from around the world always stimulates my own creativity. Quilty friends are the best!

Index